THE ACCELERATING ORGANIZATION
EMBRACING THE HUMAN FACE OF CHANGE

THE ACCELERATING ORGANIZATION EMBRACING THE HUMAN FACE OF CHANGE

Learning Acceleration

Strategic Flexibility

Change–Readiness

Hidden Leverage

Operational Alignment

Organizational Involvement

Arun Maira
Peter Scott-Morgan

McGraw-Hill
New York • San Francisco • Washington, D.C. • Auckland • Bogotá
Caracas • Lisbon • London • Madrid • Mexico City • Milan
Montreal • New Delhi • San Juan • Singapore
Sydney • Tokyo • Toronto

Library of Congress Cataloging-in-Publication Data

Maira, Arun.
    The accelerating organization : embracing the human face of change
  / Arun Maira, Peter Scott-Morgan.
        p.   cm.
    Includes index.
    ISBN 0-07-057720-X
    1. Organizational change—Management.   2. Organizational learning.
I. Scott-Morgan, Peter. II. Title.
HD58.8.M243   1996
658.4'07124—dc20   96-20996
                                                                          CIP

McGraw-Hill

A Division of The McGraw-Hill Companies

  234567890 DOC/DOC 9010987

ISBN 0-07-057720-X

The sponsoring editor for this book was *Philip Ruppel* and the production supervisor was *Don Schmidt.* It was set in Century Old Style by *TopDesk Publishers'
Group,* which was also responsible for the interior design, illustrations, and
editorial supervision.

Printed and bound by *R.R. Donnelley & Sons Company.*

McGraw-Hill books are available at special quantity discounts to use as
premiums and sales promotions, or for use in corporate training programs.
For more information, please write to the Director of Sales, McGraw-Hill,
11 West 19th Street, New York, NY 10011

 This book is printed on recycled, acid-free paper containing a minimum
of 50 percent recycled, de-inked fiber.

To Shama and Francis

CONTENTS

PREFACE

This book was born two years ago, on a bus ride from Cape Cod back to Cambridge, Massachusetts, which was fitting enough considering how much of the subsequent planning was done on the move. For the first year, whenever we happened to travel through the same place at the same time and could secure a few hours of uninterrupted conversation, we bounced ideas around: on a wonderful hike in the high mountain pastures above Évian, France, before a colloquium, in a sixteenth-century coffee house in Brussels, Belgium, before a training course, in early morning meetings at airports while we suffered from jet lag. There were the weekends and nights in offices where in the summer the air conditioning irreversibly turned itself off and in the winter the heat resolutely did the same. Through it all we talked and plotted and planned.

With the second year came the writing. And rewriting. And rewriting some more. It was a pleasant surprise for two people from different backgrounds to find they passionately shared the same beliefs. It was exhilarating to discover we could think and create in harmony, gently bouncing ill-formed ideas back and forth until they breathed and took life on the page. Through the summer of 1995 we labored weekends in Lexington and Boston's Back Bay, capped by a 14-day writing "vacation" in Devon, England, looking up from the computer screen to the sea beyond the cliffs, overworking the printer until it overheated, watching one amazing sunset after another.

Long before we decided to create a book, we had known that we shared a passionate interest in the impact people have on the performance of organizations and in the impact organizations have on the behavior of people. We were also very interested in the practical things that managers could do to leverage that connection, improving organizational performance while satisfying the people that make up the organization. But this project was possible only because of the support and input of innumerable colleagues and friends.

The ideas in this book are a synthesis of what many of us within Arthur D. Little and Innovation Associates have been working on for several years. While it's impossible to acknowledge the contribution of everyone with whom we've had the privilege of developing insights and ideas, we'd like to express our particular gratitude to Ranganath Nayak, Larry Chait, Bryan Smith, Charlie Kiefer, Fritz Bock, Nils Bohlin, Frits Lauterbach, Bob Curtice, Stu Lipoff, Hector Villaneuva, Karl Loos, Robert Hanig, and Joan Bragar. Thanks also to Celia Doremus, Kathleen Lancaster, Isobel Campbell, and Philip Ruppel and our friends at McGraw-Hill for their contributions to the production of this book.

Our special thanks to David Garvin for many hours of stimulating discussions on how organizations really learn and to Peter Senge for his inspirational ideas on personal mastery and individual learning, as well as for reviewing our manuscript.

We owe a very special word of thanks to our dear friend Robert Levering for his ideas, and another to Josh Mills for helping to pull together and refine the words in the book.

To each of you, named and unnamed, thank you!

Arun Maira
Peter Scott-Morgan
Cambridge, Massachusetts

INTRODUCTION

The pace of change is accelerating. Organizations everywhere, whether they realize it or not, are starting to compete on their ability to change faster and more effectively than their rivals. Success, sometimes survival, requires that organizations find ways to keep changing and improving.

To accomplish this—to evolve—managers need to create an accelerating organization: an organization that changes continually, skillfully and nimbly, always in alignment with its vision of the "where" it wants to be.

It is not easy. The experience that many managers have had with change programs has been discouraging. Organizational change often gets launched too late, with too little vision, leadership, planning or resources. Once under way, it generally proves difficult to control or results in unintended consequences. All this often leads to widespread change-fatigue and disillusionment. Many managers are left seeking a "silver bullet" that they hope will solve all their organizations' ills.

In general, the change programs of the last 10 years have fallen into two classes: those like Total Quality Management, which many people feel are too soft and slow, and those like Reengineering, which critics find too mechanical and invasive.

At Arthur D. Little, we surveyed 350 business executives across all major industries in the United States. Not surprisingly, each is in the throes of major change, and 80 percent expect to go through another major change within the next few years. But fewer than one sixth of those surveyed said they had achieved everything they set out to, while 40 percent expressed unhappiness with the results. A similar survey we conducted in Europe revealed a similar picture. And when we talked to the CEOs, they didn't know why their efforts had failed.

We propose a better approach to change, one that we call the Middle Way.

In our search for practical ways to manage through all the turbulence, we were struck by the organizations and the teams that have taken charge of their destinies and created the results they wanted. Their orientation was positive, creative and forward-looking, rather than reactive. It is just that path we hope to chart.

We will find a Middle Way between the apparent conflict of the hard, mechanistic and the soft, organic schools of management, drawing on the best of each. The Middle Way integrates what might seem like polar opposites: reengineering and learning, efficiency and creativity, action and emotion, strategy and implementation, bottom-line results and investment in the future.

The foundation of this Middle Way is the recognition that *the journey is the destination.* In other words, the process of change is the same as the desired outcome of that process—an organization that thrives on never-ending change. The concepts, techniques and tools that managers need to create fundamental change in the first place—that is, to convert their organization into one that can keep changing—will be the same as those they will then use to continue managing the organization. So the new school of management has to be based on an understanding of the principal components of a successful change process and the practical ways of managing them.

To provide the principles and the tools that management needs to make such changes, the subsequent sections of this book work through six components of organizational change that build an accelerating organization.

The first is **managing for strategic flexibility**. In a rapidly changing environment, the path to strategic goals must be redefined continually, even as managers nurture the core values of the organization and build upon them.

The second is **managing for change-readiness**. To galvanize action toward the organization's vision, members of the organization must be willing to leave the place they currently occupy, even if it seems comfortable. Managers will need to have a better

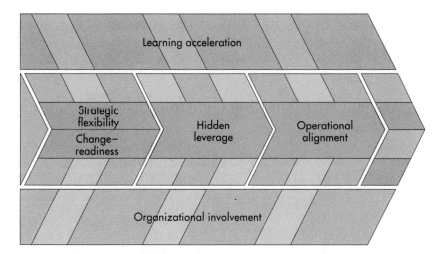

understanding of the reasons why people may resist change and will be skilled in helping people to let go of the past.

The third is **managing for hidden leverage**. This involves understanding the unwritten rules that drive the organization and finding ways to rewrite them. This can be done both by analyzing the details of how the rules work, and by "systems thinking"—stepping back for a broad analysis that helps locate the hidden leverage.

The fourth is **managing for operational alignment**. This involves creating a smooth transition from systems thinking to systems action. The challenge is to change, simultaneously and harmoniously, the many interrelated facets of the organization—management policies, organization structures, business processes and resources—without disrupting performance.

The fifth component is **managing for organizational involvement**. Change has to take place not just in planning sessions but in the minds of people and in their day-to-day actions. It's vital to involve the final implementors as early as possible—so they become the agents of change rather than the victims of change.

The sixth component is **managing for learning acceleration**. People must learn what is of most value to those on whom they rely for support: customers, colleagues, providers of capital, suppliers and others. And they must learn how to provide this value more efficiently and effectively than their existing and potential competitors. As an organization changes, it must build an infrastructure of continuous learning so that it can sustain high performance. It must encode change and learning into the very DNA of the organization.

Strategic flexibility, Change-readiness, Hidden leverage, Operational alignment, Organizational involvement, Learning acceleration. For which there is a handy acronym: **SCHOOL**...as in School of the Middle Way.

It's a school for business warriors—results-oriented, tough-minded pragmatists—fighting not just for survival but for the right to shape their futures. It's a school for business philosophers—people-oriented, progressive idealists—who seek a more enlightened approach to performance. All can benefit from learning the Middle Way, and at each step we'll examine where we stand in the process, what we have learned so far and where we hope to go next.

Nothing in this book is theoretical. It is based, in part, on our own practical experience and that of our colleagues at Arthur D. Little in guiding organizations through major change programs. This book also draws heavily on discussions with leaders and managers who have achieved transformational change or continue to seek it, as well as on discussions with academic researchers who study organizational learning, leadership, and change.

If there is one underlying principle we hold dear, it is this: *the key is people.*

Although good processes deliver results—which is the thesis of reengineering—processes don't learn. People do, and people cause processes to improve and perform. Only people can aspire to change and make change happen; no other asset of the organization can do that. Only by embracing the human face of change—training people, nurturing them, inspiring them, listening to them, leading them—can you forge an accelerating organization.

Learning Acceleration

Strategic
Flexibility

Change–
Readiness

Hidden
Leverage

Operational
Alignment

Organizational Involvement

MANAGING FOR STRATEGIC FLEXIBILITY

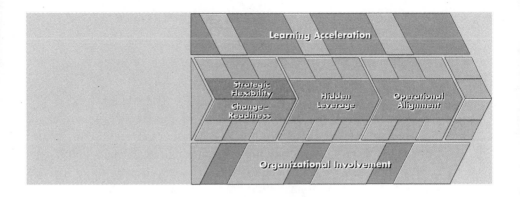

NEWTONIAN STRATEGY

Q: When is the mental model of traditional strategy still appropriate?

A: It depends.

It was 1665, a gorgeous summer's day. In his parents' garden sat a farmer's son of 23, avoiding the plague that had shut Cambridge University. An apple dropped from a tree, and Isaac Newton began to wonder why it fell straight down.

So the story goes. In 1687, Newton published a book, "Principia," which proposed mathematical laws of motion and gravity that remained uncontested for two centuries. It is generally regarded as the greatest work of science ever written. And we now know it's wrong.

By 1915, when Einstein announced the second part of his Theory of Relativity, the nicely mechanistic universe of Newton was being consigned to the idealogical attic. Time, it had been learned, could dilate at high velocities; matter could convert to energy. Quantum mechanics and its relativism now explained a world beyond Newtonian mechanics.

■ CHANGING THE SHAPE OF STRATEGIC THINKING

Other models of the universe we have in our heads pose the same problem: They work so well that we believe they're fundamentally correct. When too much evidence comes along that doesn't fit our mental model, we feel forced to adopt a new one, a model that can accommodate all the available data—at least for a while.

The pace of change, reflected in both external and internal pressures, is forcing more managers in more organizations to question and modify their mental models. However, all that questioning and modifying can undermine employees' confidence in the strategy makers. So, many top managers must ask not just "should we radically change the shape of our strategic thinking?" but "*how* should we radically change the shape of our strategic thinking?"

Let's not forget that mainstream strategic thinking is not likely to give way overnight to radical alternatives. In fact, for some organizations, the Newtonian strategic thinking that people have been using for the last few decades may remain adequate for the next few as well.

The old strategy still works if these conditions prevail:

- Change in the environment is slow.
- Competitors are easily identifiable.
- Environmental variables are few.

For how many organizations does this still apply? Not many.

Just consider a few conditions we're all aware of. Microsoft is being considered a competitive threat to banks; Harley Davidson is realizing that some of its main competitors are Range Rover and power boat manufacturers; in telecommunications, it's hard to keep track of who's competing with whom.

The global interconnections go well beyond the Internet. With declining trade barriers, blurring industrial boundaries and closely connected financial markets, change on one side of the world causes almost immediate ramifications on the other. The problems in the Mexican economy, for example, affected many countries within days—in Asia as well as in North and South America.

But before embarking on the quest for a radically new way to shape strategy, we should study what we want to change. So let's take stock of the traditional view of strategy.

Conceptually, strategy is all about making optimal choices of products, markets and ways of competing, based on analyzing the business environment, gaining insights into the moves of competitors and predicting the consequences of one's choices. Metaphorically, it's a competitive battlefield where the underlying mental model is the zero-sum game—you win or you're vanquished.

Newtonian strategy development is based on highly intelligent people at the top of an organization working through Data Gathering, Analysis, Selection and Planning, then passing the results to others to implement. Classically, top managers are not intimately involved in all the activities.

In the Data Gathering phase, a strategy group—perhaps supported by external strategy consultants or market research firms—obtains information about the business environment, the industry, competitors and so on. With little input from top management, the group moves on to Analysis, using its favorite strategy model to structure data in order to guide executives to make informed decisions.

At the Selection phase, the top managers get heavily involved, selecting their preferred strategy and instructing the strategy group to flesh it out. The Planning phase is largely a question of producing detailed versions of the strategy document, with top management now largely in review mode.

Yet in the search for sustained corporate performance, maybe there's as much leverage in improving top management performance—in strategy making, for example—as there is in reengineering the work of middle managers and TQMing the work of operators.

The old-style Newtonian approaches to strategy did not include organizational learning, nor did they have to. Because they weren't intended to change the organization into one that could keep changing. But if change is our goal, we must note that today's vision statements, strategies and business objectives rarely help organizations become accelerated learning organizations.

Vision statements tend to be pie-in-the-sky and bland. The strategies tend to be intellectually neat but abstract, so people in the body of the company don't see the implications for themselves. Business objectives, usually stated in financial terms, are often utterly uninspiring.

To be truly effective, strategy must be a lot more than just a neat construct. It must reflect the vision of the external world, the internal world and the journey to realize the goal, and it must inspire the entire organization to take that journey. The whole vision, strategy and objectives must be cast to galvanize the troops, inspiring a battalion to take a hill under heavy fire and plant its flag on top. Taking the hill will reinforce the sense of teamwork and the validity of the strategy. It will also accelerate the push to achieve the vision.

The challenge to business leaders is to shape and communicate vision, strategy and objectives that resonate among the people—in the minds of those who have to put them into practice. To do this, strategy needs to reflect the human face of change. Management needs to spell out goals that people believe in and are inspired to reach. So they need to create not just ambition-driven strategies but also emotional strategies. What we're talking about is developing cutting-edge strategies that involve people.

And the way to do that is with what we call "Relativistic Strategy." To us this denotes a nimble and dynamic style of management, in which goals are always tied to aspirations and refined as aspirations change, whether of necessity or by design.

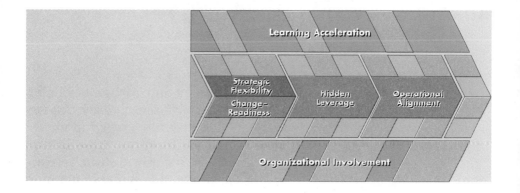

RELATIVISTIC STRATEGY

On the evening of September 30, 1859, a 50-year-old lawyer addressed the Wisconsin State Agricultural Society, in Milwaukee:

"It is said an Eastern monarch once charged his wise men to invent him a sentence to be ever in view, and which should be true and appropriate in all times and situations. They presented him with the words: 'And this, too, shall pass away!'"

The lawyer was Abraham Lincoln, and those words are as profound today as they were then.

Just a few years ago, Royal Dutch/Shell asked its strategic planners, "In a world of change, how can we cope?" When they reported back, they presented a list of innovative approaches to strategy that cutting-edge firms had adopted during the 1970s. "That's all very well," replied the Shell executives, "but how do we know that those approaches work? Look for examples with a bit more track record."

The planners eventually decided to look at every firm that had been around for more than a century, to see what they might learn from the variety of strategies that the firms had adopted to endure. They found 40 firms from Europe, the United States and Japan, several of which had histories stretching back more than 200 years. The oldest was Stora of Sweden, which, with a 700-year history, was almost as old as Methuselah. More chillingly, the planners found the average life expectancy of firms to be less than 50 years.

So what was common in the strategy of the longest-enduring firms? First, they were conservative in financing, leaving themselves room to maneuver when the world changed in unpredictable ways. Second, their top management was active in society—not necessarily High Society, but inquisitive about developments in a variety of fields. Third, there was always a strong sense of identity and cohesion within the organizations. "Who are we?" always brought a clear answer, even if the company changed its core business (Stora, for instance, went from copper mining to chemicals to forestry to paper). And fourth, the Methuselah firms had great tolerance for experimentation at their margins—and tried neither to control the experiment nor insist that all the probing at the margins be relevant to the core businesses.

 SCENARIO PLANNING REFERENCE

The Royal Dutch/Shell approach to create scenarios for planning was described in depth by Peter Schwartz in "The Art of the Long View" (New York: Doubleday, 1991).

From these historical successes, we can suggest some processes for developing a strategy that break with traditional approaches and reflect a world in flux—a relativistic strategy. Always, the keys are to be nimble, to be prepared to rethink plans and to tie your goals directly to your aspirations.

First, scan the environment more broadly than in the past.

Second, reflect with an open mind on any emerging patterns.

Third, nurture the ability to be flexible, to infuse the strategy process with aspiration and ambition—a positive energy for change. Otherwise, the strategy development will result in an intellectually neat, philosophically correct strategy that remains sitting on a shelf in the CEO's office.

Fourth, reinforce—even codify, if necessary—the constants of the organization, so that people have a guiding light to provide them with security and comfort as they apply ever-changing, and often ambiguous, new strategies.

Finally, engage those responsible for implementation in the strategy development.

The result of these steps will be a reflective, engaging, emergent process, as opposed to the traditional analytic, directive, planned process. In the words of one of our clients, the overriding goal for relativistic strategy is to: "Apply the mind and grab the gut."

Let's now look at each of these processes.

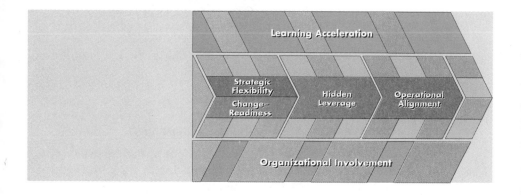

SURVEILLANCE

Scanning the environment is really a continuous process, a stream that in turn feeds other processes: sharing understanding, committing to choices, engagement.

As you scan, remember that three fundamental principles underlie the process:

- You can't predict the future, but you can see trends and anticipate possible scenarios.
- You can't create scenarios for everything, so focus on issues that are very important to you.
- You need to explore the scenarios from the viewpoint of everyone likely to have a vested interest in your organization.

Even if people can't predict the future, they have an innate ability to see patterns and connections, and that's the skill needed when scanning environments. Essential to this process is recognizing the strong connections among various trends and then creating possible scenarios.

Then, with the scenarios in view, managers need to explore them from the points of view of all key stakeholders—customers, investors, employees, suppliers, the community. What are their needs, and how can you satisfy them?

Why bother? Because there is strong evidence that sustained high performance is correlated with the balanced satisfaction of the needs of all the stakeholders. Focusing on satisfying the owners of the business by pursuing profit to the exclusion of all else does not provide sustainable growth.*

 STAKERHOLDER-NEEDS REFERENCE

Probably the most comprehensive evidence of the importance of balancing stakeholder needs is presented in "Corporate Culture and Performance" (New York: Free Press, 1992), by John P. Kotter and James L. Heskett of Harvard Business School.

The same, by the way, is true in the public sector. One of us recently testified before the United States Congress about how the public sector could zero in on success when profit was not an available measure. The answer? As in the private sector, success comes from satisfying each major stakeholder of the organization, in this case the people who consume its services both internally and externally and the general public as its owners.

Honda provides a striking case study of how a company benefits from this anticipation of stakeholder needs. In the 1980s, Honda was looking at the Indian market, which at the time was closed to foreign car producers. Honda knew that India, with its large population and base of engineering capabililities, could become an important center for marketing and production operations, should it ever open its doors. Two key stakeholders in the situation were the Indian Government, and perhaps less obviously, an Indian company that might expect to form a joint venture with any foreign auto maker allowed in.

So Honda management played out scenarios from the points of view of these and other stakeholders. How would a confluence of interests come about? What could be the key factors to bring this about? What trends would have an impact on these factors?

Honda uncovered these trends: the Indian economy was being opened gradually; the Nehru dynasty was a source of future heads of Government; Prime Minister Indira Gandhi was firmly established and grooming her younger son, Sanjay, as her successor; but should Rajiv Gandhi, the eldest son, ever succeed his mother, the market for cars could quickly be opened, because he was known to be less doctrinaire on economic nationalism than either the leftist or rightist political parties. Having explored these scenarios, Honda made contingency plans and waited.

And look what unfolded: Indira Gandhi's younger son died in an air crash. Mrs. Gandhi herself was shockingly assassinated. Rajiv Gandhi became Prime Minister far more quickly than anyone had foreseen.

Some of these events were completely unanticipated. Yet Honda's analysis had foreseen a possible convergence of trends in which Rajiv Gandhi might assume leadership.

And within a few weeks of becoming Prime Minister, emboldened by the wave of sympathy for him after his mother's murder, Rajiv Gandhi announced the opening of the Indian market to foreign producers—as Honda had anticipated he might. One day later, a representative from Honda showed up at the office of the CEO of the largest Indian company with an offer of collaboration.

Scanning the environment produced a big dividend in readiness for growth.

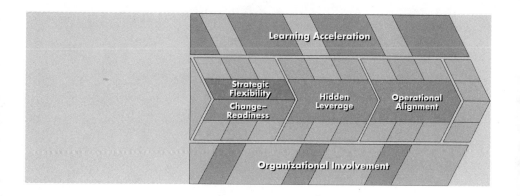

COMPLEXITY THEORY AND PRACTICE

How do we learn from what Honda did in India? How can we develop similarly useful scenarios?

We use a four-phase approach to simplifying the world into scenarios: decide the appropriate scope of the planning process; within that scope, uncover the trends in the environment likely to have an impact on your organization; create skeleton scenarios and ensure that they're internally consistent and relevant; flesh the scenarios out until they're usable.

 ## THE FOUR PHASES OF SCENARIO PLANNING

Phase 1: DECIDE SCOPE
What important decisions are facing you?

Who has a vested interest in the outcome?

What time scale is of most relevance?

Phase 2: UNCOVER TRENDS
What trends are you confident about?

What trends are you uncertain about?

What trends matter?

Phase 3:   CREATE SKELETON SCENARIOS
What themes emerge from combining trends?

How consistent are the assumptions?

How relevant are the outcomes?

How can the scenarios be refined?

Phase 4:   FLESH OUT SCENARIOS
What extra research can we do?

Can computer models help?

What would signal these scenarios?

Are the scenarios understandable to others?

■ HOW TO BUILD SCENARIOS

In the first phase, Decide Scope, the goal for your management team is to identify which decisions your organization needs to make that will influence the long-term future of the company, who has a vested interest in the outcome and what time scale to apply.

Those with a vested interest obviously include key stakeholders—but also potential competitors, governments and other key players.

The second phase of scenario planning is to Uncover Trends. Here you pull in a group of 10 to 20 experts in a variety of disciplines—science, technology, socioeconomics, politics—to identify the basic trends that will affect the issues determined by the first phase. Be rigorous in noting and categorizing those trends of which everyone is confident, in contrast to all the others. Confident doesn't always mean absolutely certain, but it often means "Certain enough to stake my career on." You may have to. Those trends that are less certain need to be noted as such—and note, too, when they rapidly degrade into immensely complex uncertain trends.

Finally, you must take a stab at which trends really matter. High-impact events that are nevertheless highly uncertain represent the cornerstones of scenarios.

The third phase is to Create Skeleton Scenarios. Here it's best to let your intuition play a larger role (in psychological terms, right brain taking precedence over left brain). Create some interesting stories around how the various elements might interact under certain conditions.

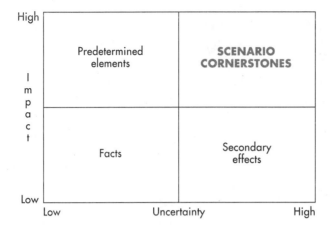

If you need a stimulus, try lumping all the worst-case trends together, and then all the best-case trends. Or choose a category such as Major Disconnects or Dangers and see what stories you can build using the trends you uncovered in Phase 2. Give the stories evocative titles such as "Everyone Loves Us!" or "People Want to be Couch Potatoes." These stories are the bones of skeleton scenarios.

As the stories get richer, check them for consistency and relevance. Are there mutually inconsistent trends acting as foundations for the story—zero inflation as well as full employment, for example? Is the likely behavior of all of those with vested interests being fully reflected? Are the scenarios unstable? If they are, push the story a stage further to reveal the eventual outcome. And finally, is the story relevant, given the scope determined in Phase 1?

When you can tell a rich and believable story that has relevant implications to your organization, you have created a skeleton scenario. For Honda, this was "India Opens Doors."

The final phase of scenario planning is to flesh out what you have. Maybe you need more data on potential market size, reactions of key players, financial impact, and so on. Maybe computer modeling and simulation can help you explore the scenario.

When you're happy with the scenarios, it's essential to do two things: set up an early warning system to show you when one is on its way, and ensure that people who weren't in the room when you derived the scenarios will understand them—and understand them in the same way as those who were in the room. Then you've finished the scanning portion of your Relativistic Strategy development.

■ COMMON MISTAKES IN SCENARIO PLANNING

During this process, people commonly make two basic mistakes: They rely on input from too narrow a group of people, or they curtail the process too early. Both can be fatal.

You would expect that the first problem would be easy to avoid. Surely the solution is just to invite a wide range of experts. But all too often companies rely on satisfaction data from their present stakeholders to indicate how well they're performing. Stakeholders can change, and the needs of current stakeholders can change. Digital Equipment Corporation (DEC), for example, assumed that the customers for its computers would continue to be corporations. Ken Olson, then the company's president, stated in 1977 that he saw "No reason for any individual to have a computer in their home."(Oh, well....) DEC couldn't imagine that its corporate customers' needs could be met by personal computers. So it measured the satisfaction of its customers with its excellent minicomputers and, as a result, was lulled into believing that it was setting the standards in the industry and that no change was warranted. It recognized its delusion too late.

The moral of that story is: Most employee and customer satisfaction surveys are measures of what has happened already—not a projection into new possibilities.

The other common mistake organizations make in scenario planning is to curtail the process too early. This problem shows itself under a number of guises, all of them apparently legitimate. The first is the "Let's make sure that we're really focused" approach, which can lead the group, from Phase 1 onward, to look only at one or two scenarios. This approach smacks of prediction where no prediction may be possible. How can you know which one or two scenarios might be the relevant ones?

Phase 2 brings its own problems of premature narrowing. Here, as soon as they've identified a basic trend, some planners get so excited by the chase that they take off into the likely implications of the trend and possible actions for each implication. They need to stay cool and let all the trends emerge.

For some, completing Phase 3 feels like such a creative, intuitive, right-brain sort of a thing, and such a demonstration of ability to keep the normally dominant other half of their cortex in check, that with unselfconscious abandon they unleash their logical left brains to devour the juicy morsels they've just prepared. "Let's Act Now!" their frustrated portside neurons fire in a concerted synaptic volley, for which few results-oriented managers have a defense.

This is unfortunate. Failure to flesh out the scenarios and agree on the early signals to look for is like installing a highly sophisticated security system without wiring up all the sensors.

Again, observe the Honda model. Management constructed rich narratives about how the world could get from its current situation to "India Opens Doors." The departure of Indira Gandhi from the Prime Ministership in a way that would enable her son Rajiv, rather than a leftist opponent, to succeed her was a signal. When this signal was noted, Honda realized that the scenario in which India could become a major Asian auto center was likely to emerge sooner rather than later.

On the other side of the ledger, consider a major bank that invited a bunch of experts to help with scenario planning on whether it needed to acquire capabilities in information technology. The experts were drawn from fields the bank felt were important: information systems, banking regulations, the banking industry. Each expert in turn steered the discussion to the implications of the trends in his or her area of expertise and to the measures the bank could take to counter those trends. It proved difficult to get anyone to take a step back.

When a set of scenarios did eventually emerge, almost everyone, including the CEO, immediately expressed a preference. A bias for action surfaced, much too soon in the process. A lonely voice spoke up: "How can we scan the environment to validate if any of the scenarios are emerging? What will be the signals?" The voice was ignored. In the months ahead, everyone gathered evidence only for the scenario they preferred. They couldn't detect or interpret the signals that an alternative scenario might be emerging because they didn't know what those signals would be. They'd never built up the stories of the scenarios. They were blind.

If you ever feel tempted to rely solely on your unaided intuition, if you feel so experienced that scenario planning is simply a waste of time, remember the last words of General John B. Sedgwick at the Battle of Spotsylvania in 1864: "They couldn't hit an elephant at this dist . . . AHHH!"

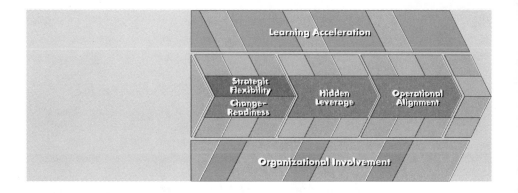

COLLECTIVE COGNITION

In the spirit of the Middle Way, when you gather a team to develop and discuss scenarios, you must find the right balance between open-ended dialogue and forced-closure discussion. It's what we think of as a Productive Conversation.

For instance, you need to come to a series of closures, such as agreeing on a range of skeleton scenarios, and usually you have a time limit. But you don't need to reach any form of closure at each meeting, and you shouldn't be tempted to hurry the process along. Indeed, you'll probably move faster in the long run if the meetings take longer (a few hours, at least), yet are richer than normal.

Overall, you'd prefer that people remain focused—but not all the time. Everyone may feel they have something to contribute, but they must also be eager to understand everyone else's perspective. Everyone should talk—and listen far more than they typically do. Then they should play back what they think they heard to confirm understanding. Yes, this takes some time. But it provides the richest possible result.

PRODUCTIVE CONVERSATIONS REFERENCE

Some of the best of these techniques, advocated by Innovation Associates, an Arthur D. Little company, are included in "The Fifth Discipline Fieldbook" (New York: Doubleday, 1994), by Peter M. Senge, Art Kleiner, Charlotte Roberts, Richard B. Ross and Bryan J. Smith.

People should feel they can challenge what others say. Discussing some issues may be embarrassing, but that isn't a reason not to discuss them, nor should there be any form of retribution for raising them.

Often, there will be different levels of seniority and different turfs represented in the group, but everyone must agree to act as if they were respectful colleagues. Although some people may have fundamental disagreements, they shouldn't argue. Instead, they should explore whether their mental models are different. Finally, even if there are times when people get frustrated or angry, they should try to analyze why they feel as they do and share that reasoning with the group.

Everyone who attends the scenario planning sessions should agree to abide by this protocol of productive conversations. The term *protocol* is an accurate one—this is literally a form of etiquette.

The protocol of productive conversations

• We must eventually reach closure	• Not every meeting need reach closure
• We have an overall time limit	• Meetings should be longer but richer
• Overall we should remain focused	• We should allow for related diversions
• We bring an important perspective	• Contrary viewpoints should be explored.
• We must each talk	• We shouldn't interrupt but listen more
• We each bring a lot of experience	• None of us alone knows what is best
• Some people will say silly things	• We shouldn't ridicule others, but inquire further
• We should challenge what others say	• We should test our own and others' assumptions
• Some issues are embarrassing	• We should agree to explore difficult issues
• Different seniorities/turfs will be present	• Seniority/turf should be left at the door
• We may fundamentally disagree	• Disagreement should be seen as the source of new thinking.
• We may get frustrated or angry	• We should share why we feel as we do

The fundamental premise of a meeting designed to encourage deep-shared understanding is respect: candor with your colleagues, respect for their ideas, politeness when you disagree.

This approach, by the way, is similar to that of the native North Americans, who historically have held open discussions, without attempting to reach closure, until a common feeling of what to do emerges naturally. It is also intriguingly similar to the Quaker decision-making process where each member of the group is honor bound to explain any differences in view he or she has on a particular issue, and action is taken only when the whole meeting has reached unity.

But time is indeed limited. So what can you do to speed the process of exploration, discovery and insight? Being clear about the firm's values and its vision is essential.

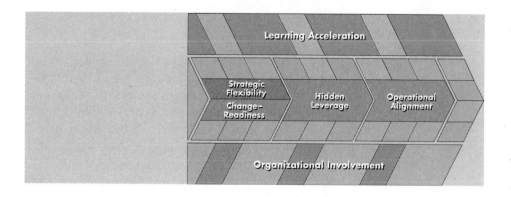

INTEGRAL VALUES

HOW BIG BLUE BLEW IT

When Thomas Watson Jr. set forth his views on IBM, he stressed that its basic philosophy of doing business was giving full consideration to the individual employee, spending a lot of time making customers happy and going the last mile to do things right. Everything else, he emphasized, should be permanently up for grabs. In the late 1980s and early 1990s, IBM appeared to forget this advice. By emphasizing noncore values such as a dress code, insisting on the importance of mainframes and accepting the legitimacy of fiefdoms, it stumbled badly.

There's a lot of saccharine in the word *values*, so much so that it's at risk of becoming devalued by overuse. But let us reject such debasement of the term generally and understand, pragmatically, what makes values important.

As organizations cultivate the ability to change constantly, how can the corporate ship be kept stable? Through core values, which act as stabilizers when the sea of change becomes turbulent.

Royal Dutch/Shell's study of Methuselah firms found that all had a strong sense of identity beyond the business they were in or their technological competencies. A more recent study by James Collins and Jerry Porras ("Built to Last," Harper Business,

1994) went further. It compared the most respected high-performing companies in a variety of industries with another successful company in the same industry: Johnson & Johnson with Bristol-Myers Squibb, Merck with Pfizer, General Electric with Westinghouse, Sony with Kenwood, Procter & Gamble with Colgate, Hewlett-Packard with Texas Instruments, and so on. All the companies had been in business for at least 50 years, but the focus of the research was not why the companies survived; it was why the higher-performing company did better than its counterpart.

Their conclusion? The leading firms had stronger and more enduring core values. These values did not just appear on a plaque in the entrance hall but were what the organization was managed by. One of Sony's core values, for example, is to be a pioneer, not following others but doing what seems impossible. A Motorola core value is continuous self renewal; at Wal-Mart, one was swimming upstream, against conventional wisdom.

Closely linked with values was the expression of the purpose of the firm. In none of the leading companies was the making of profits the stated principal purpose—although all the firms made more profits than the counterpart firms.

Note how important this is: Merely making a profit does not bring out the best in people; indeed, it can divide members of the firm as much as it unites them in their common pursuit. Some firms on Wall Street, with their tunnel vision on profits, have become travesties of what great organizations can be.

■ ENHANCING CORE VALUES

But managers can't concoct a new set of core values as they go along. The core values, chosen and expressed as a philosophy by which to live and do business, are stabilizers, and you disregard them at your peril. So a Relativistic Strategy must reflect and reinforce the core values, not try to change them.

Now any, or all, of the specific manifestations of the core values can and should be changed, but not the core values themselves. This proves confusing to many managers.

Modifying core values is not like replacing one set of stabilizers with better ones. It's like seeing a storm approaching, taking the old stabilizers and throwing them away, then starting to build new stabilizers from scratch.

So how do you determine what the operating values of your organization are? They may not be what it says on your organization's value statement—if there is one. They may not even be what employees say they are. But they are revealed by how the organization and its people act.

In practice, there is no such thing as "corporate" values—only the *shared values of the individuals* whom the corporation comprises. Core values are the sum of what motivates people (as discussed in Chapter 3), the common denominator of what is important to the individuals in the organization. So core values relate to what encourages people to go to work on a Monday morning, what engages them, what gains them respect, what creates pride in belonging, what makes them feel worthy.

That's why it is so dangerous to disregard core values. Companies that try to do so are effectively telling their employees, "You personally value X, but you're wrong!" There is no evidence that what is important to people can be changed even under duress, so denying core corporate values only creates frustration and erodes morale. Core values cannot be denied, only transformed.

What is most important to each of us does tend to evolve over time—just consider what was really important to you at age 10, 20 and 30. So organizations can legitimately choose to strongly reinforce aspects of their existing values, in order, for example, to create a "quality culture" or a "customer-focused mindset." But it is naive to propose new corporate values that don't build on values already held at the individual level, and it is dangerous to deny values that do. In each case, the new values may be worthy in the abstract—but they simply don't fit with the reality of the people who make up the organization.

Recognizing that core values are the shared values of individuals gives a clue as to how these values can be reinforced or transformed: by repeatedly demonstrating, to the organization and to the world, that the desired values will be upheld at any cost.

Consider Johnson & Johnson, whose value statement declares that the firm's first responsibility is to all those who use its products. In 1982, seven people in the Chicago area took the analgesic Tylenol and died within minutes. Somebody had tampered with their Tylenol bottles and laced them with cyanide. J&J immediately recalled every Tylenol capsule in the United States, even though only the Chicago area appeared to be affected. They also mounted a massive campaign to alert the public. The estimated

Phases in Newtonian strategy development

Processes in relativistic strategy development

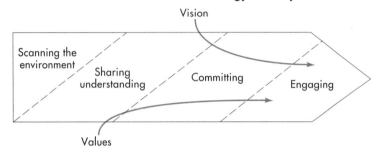

cost was $100 million. The response came easily, because J&J relied on its core values.

Organizational values feed into Relativistic Strategy development particularly through the process of sharing, understanding and committing.

Consider Tata, a large Indian company that in the late 1970s created a division in a part of the country where it previously had no operations. Management declared to the new workforce that its values included not just maintaining high quality but providing work places where every individual would be treated with dignity and respect. No matter how serious the differences of opinion, it declared, they would be resolved by nonviolent, open and honest discussion.

At the time, this was unheard of in that part of the country. Industrial strife was commonplace; quality was variable.

One day, the general manager of the new Tata division upbraided an employee on the factory floor. No one saw anything unusual about the incident. But one employee wrote to the CEO and asked if that type of interaction was consistent with the values of respect and dignity that the company hoped to create.

The CEO called the general manager and asked what their response should be, and they agreed that the general manager had flouted the stated values. The next day, the general manager publicly apologized to the employee and to the organization for not having honored the corporate values. The story became legend. In the 1980s, a communist group infiltrated the Tata union and disrupted collective bargaining for a wage agreement. Property was damaged, managers were abused. The law gave Tata little room for maneuver; it couldn't make any layoffs without the written permission of the Government. The managers declared that they would stick to their corporate values: They would not allow the workers to breach the values of respect and dignity that the company sought; they would shut the division.

Everyone was told that they would continue to be paid, but they couldn't come to work.

Within three days, the workers, gathering in their own communities, agreed that the onus was on them to reaffirm the corporate values. They threw out the union troublemakers. The division at once reopened. Production shortfalls were made up. In the following months, quality rose and absenteeism dropped. The values were stronger than ever.

The values had stabilized Tata through the storm.

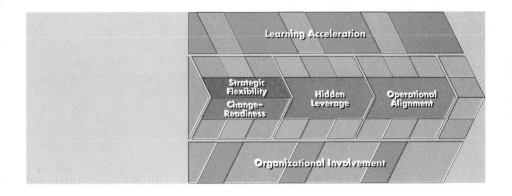

Learning Acceleration

Strategic Flexibility
Change-Readiness

Hidden Leverage

Operational Alignment

Organizational Involvement

GUIDED BY THE LIGHT

If corporate values provide the stabilizers during a storm, corporate vision provides the point of reference on the horizon, a beacon of light. The right form of vision is vital to prepare for the new strategy—and it need not take forever to produce.

For a vision to be worth anything, it must have three components. First, it must specify Aspiration, a unique long-term achievement that the organization is striving for. Second, it must offer Inspiration, which acts as a supermagnet, pulling the organization onward and upward through change. Third, it must invite Perspiration, suggesting how the people in the organization can bring that achievement closer every day.

Most "vision statements" don't satisfy these criteria, because they seem to focus on taking some pithy thoughts and casting them in stone. Their focus, unfortunately, is on the statement rather than on the vision.

To be useful, a vision must be the highest-level component of our Relativistic Strategy, a beacon when almost everything else is changing. You change the vision infrequently, but you do change it as you start getting close to achieving it. The core values of your organization, in contrast, have to act as a foundation to every vision because you tamper with them at your peril. So, conceptually, values come before a vision.

Another, less lofty image of vision is as a brochure for the next leg of the voyage, focusing on where you want to go, how you plan to get there and what the attractions of the trip might be.

A brochure would be useless if the destinations all sounded the same, or if it tried to attract people with nothing more inspiring than the promise that the voyage wouldn't cost too much. But don't think the description of a vision must go on and on. Keep it crisp and memorable.

 SMALL IS BEAUTIFUL

Komatsu, a small Japanese manufacturer of earth-moving equipment, was trying to come up with a vision. The main competitor was Caterpillar, which was many times larger. Management decided its long-term aspiration was to stand up to Caterpillar, though they were too small to take it on head to head. The strategy was to box Caterpillar in selected markets. How could they sum up this vision? Two words: Encircle Caterpillar. (If you can describe your vision in less, you win the prize.) Because Komatsu employees understood the vision, they could read a lot into those two words and understand what flowed from the vision.

■ PRAGMATIC ROUTES TO A SHARED VISION

Given the importance of a useful vision, what's the best way of developing one? Should you involve everyone? Or should a small number of you lock yourselves away, come up with a vision, and then lobby for its acceptance? Let's find the Middle Way.

After searching long and hard, we found happiness in the framework used by Bryan Smith of Innovation Associates. He has found five routes to a shared vision:

TELLING: The CEO creates a vision and advises the organization to follow it.

SELLING: The CEO believes in a vision and encourages the organization to follow it.

TESTING: The CEO has some ideas about a vision and gets the organization's reaction.

CONSULTING: To put together a vision, the CEO gets creative input from the organization.

CO-CREATING: Together, the CEO and the rest of the organization create a shared vision.

The five approaches fit five different sets of circumstances. As you move down the list from Telling to Co-creating, each approach requires more involvement, which in turn requires greater skills in direction setting and organizational learning. For many organizations, pulling off Co-creating will be difficult, because it requires skills that most companies don't have. In contrast, many organizations could cope with the Telling route, because that approach primarily requires a strong leader.

Nevertheless, what one considers the best approach at first should not necessarily remain the preferred approach.

Overall, Co-creating is probably the most resilient approach for creating a shared vision, and therefore may be the approach to aim for in the long term; most accelerating organizations will probably use Co-creating. If you're not yet an accelerating organization, use the approach that fits your needs, but hone your skills so that you can improve on the approach when the time comes to revisit your vision.

Here are Bryan Smith's tips on the five approaches.

Telling: You need it during a crisis, when top management is pressured to make dramatic change. Although it's a classic command-and-control approach, it can produce a vision that inspires everyone.

The key is to inform people clearly, directly and consistently, filling in all the details of why the change needs to be made. On the one hand, you must tell the truth about the organization; on the other, you must not build the vision on those negative aspects. The vision should be an aspiration.

Make it clear whether anything in the vision is negotiable. If not, say so clearly. Then let the organization fill in the details; if you provide all the details, there's nothing left for others to contribute to make the vision their own.

Selling: To sell a vision you need open channels of communication. You also take a leap of faith: You need to believe that once you explain your statement, others will see its attraction for themselves. As a result, you have to reassure people that if they all end up disagreeing with you, it will make a difference. Otherwise, you might as well be in Telling mode.

To sell your vision, you need to focus on what is important to people throughout the organization. And you need to show how it ties into what is important to you as well.

Finally, be careful that people aren't saying "Yes" under duress. You may think they're behind you, and you may be right—or you may soon feel a metaphorical knife between your shoulder blades.

Testing: In Testing, you lay out your vision not just to see if people support it, but to see which bits they support most, which least, and what you can do to improve it. You have to supply as much background material as possible and highlight all the implications, including any negative ones.

Do everything to improve the quality of responses, including ensuring anonymity for feedback.

Don't test the vision only with questionnaires—you won't pick up the subtleties you will in face-to-face interviews.

Consulting: A great approach for creating a vision if you know that you don't have all the answers yourself. The best method seems to be to set the ground rules by which the visioning exercise will proceed and then cascade the discussion down the organization, building in safeguards against distortion.

Many organizations use videos of the CEO to kick off the meeting. But this can go wrong if the video isn't updated as a result of feedback from discussion. In any case, make sure that someone collects anonymous written comments at the end of each session.

Some managers worry that if they ask people to suggest ideas, they will be flooded with options. That might well happen. And if you worry that your organization is not yet capable of coordinating the feedback, Testing may be a better approach.

Co-creating: In this most advanced form of visioning, everyone in the organization starts by creating his or her own personal vision. Some managers worry that this is a dangerous starting point, because personal visions are likely to be misaligned. Yet if they are, you have a problem anyway.

The aim is for teams to articulate their sense of common purpose. Then, teams that are interdependent align their visions. The goal is alignment and compatibility—not uniformity. Eventually, all the visions combine to create a hierarchy of aligned visions for the organization as a whole.

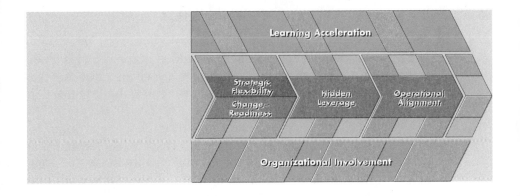

Learning Acceleration

Strategic Flexibility

Change-Readiness

Hidden Leverage

Operational Alignment

Organizational Involvement

WHERE DO YOU START?

As you work to develop Relativistic Strategy, in what order should you progress through the phases of scanning, sharing understanding, committing, engaging, visioning and considering values? Or, put another way, where do you start?

The honest answer is probably anywhere and perhaps everywhere. All these processes are required together. Of course, in any particular cycle, committing must emerge from understanding, and understanding from scanning. But vision can create new possibilities, especially if it's an aspiration-driven vision.

What about the role of the strategic planning group in all this? The role will have to change. The strategic planning group in an accelerating organization is not there to make and communicate strategy, but to enable the organization to create and become committed to innovative strategies. The group's new role is to make the organization aware of how the strategy process works, and to create conditions to enable the process to happen. That role is in partnership with the CEO and other functional enablers such as the human resources and information systems departments.

The group can best play the role by providing techniques and tools, and by encouraging reflection about the strategy so that the process can be improved—in other words, so that the organization can learn.

The inspirational supermagnet embedded in the vision is a key to helping your organization embrace the vision. But more is needed—a whole series of magnets throughout the organization to help pull it onward and upward.

You need a process by which groups throughout your organization can detail the aspects that they are responsible for and that they understand. You need a process of engaging the entire organization, of converting the big goals of the strategy into goals that each person will strive for. So you need something more sophisticated than a process merely for your planning department to convert the vision and strategies into plans that the CEO must then Tell or Sell to the organization.

Such a process is intimately tied to managing for change-readiness. That's where we'll turn next.

SIGNPOSTS TO MANAGING FOR STRATEGIC FLEXIBILITY

If you feel disoriented on the strategic Middle Way, use these points of reference to get your bearings:

1. Strategic thinking based on a Newtonian, mechanistic view is increasingly irrelevant. It is based on premises that will apply less and less in the future as the pace of change accelerates.

2. Relativistic Strategy is based on three fundamental Uncertainty Principles:

   • You can't predict the future, but you can see trends and anticipate possible scenarios.

   • You can't create scenarios for everything, so you need to focus on issues that are most important to you.

   • You need to explore those scenarios from the viewpoint of everyone likely to have a vested interest in your organization.

3. The Relativistic Strategy process must engage those charged with implementing it; the process must grab both their hearts and minds.

4. Develop scenarios with a view to accelerating organizational learning—and to understanding the implications of significant trends.

5. Become skillful as a team. Learn to reach decisions that everyone is committed to.

6. In an increasingly turbulent world, remember that Core Values are the stabilizers of the organization.

7. A corporation's core values are the common denominator of the values of individual employees.

8. Values are reinforced—or even created—when they are visibly followed. That's all the more true when adherence to values hurts the bottom line in the short term.

9. Select the approach to creating a vision that best fits the circumstances of your organization. Among the choices:

   • CEO creates a vision and advises organization to follow it

   • CEO believes in vision and encourages organization to follow it

   • CEO has ideas about vision and gets organization's reaction

   • CEO seeks creative input from organization to create a vision

   • CEO and rest of organization create a shared vision

10. The role of the strategy group in an organization must be to catalyze and coach the strategy development process—not to develop strategic plans.

11. A useful expression of a vision must have three components:

    Aspiration: specifies unique long-term achievement to strive for

    Inspiration: acts on the organization as a supermagnet

    Perspiration: suggests how every day the achievement can be brought closer

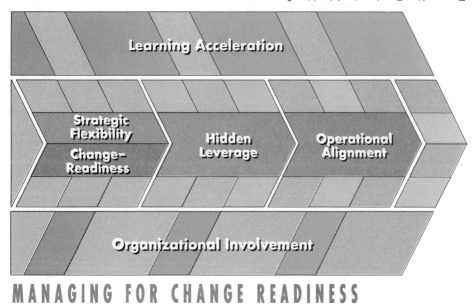

MANAGING FOR CHANGE READINESS

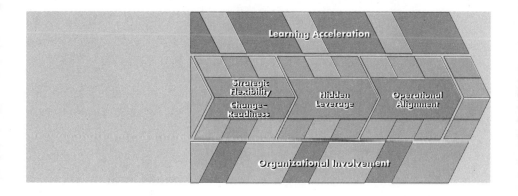

Learning Acceleration

Strategic Flexibility

Change-Readiness

Hidden Leverage

Operational Alignment

Organizational Involvement

CRITERIA FOR CHANGE-READINESS

Is change-readiness simply a question of inspiring people? No. In fact, there are five basic criteria for change-readiness.

People throughout the organization must feel that:

- Change is necessary
- The proposed change is appropriate
- As individuals, they have been acknowledged
- They have the skills to achieve the goals
- The "system" supports the required behavior

All five criteria have to be met for an organization to achieve the widespread dynamic tension that is needed to transform it. Failure to meet any one criterion acts as the weakest link in a chain and causes the whole initiative to fall apart.

The process of managing for change-readiness is, in fact, remarkably like preparing for a mountain-climbing expedition— and comparable in difficulty, although it is careers, not lives, that will be at stake.

Each member of the mountaineering team needs to feel that the climb is necessary, that the selected route is the best, that everyone will be acknowledged, that the team feels competent, and that the support system is appropriate. They must accept the challenge of scaling a peak "because it's there," as the mountaineer George Lee Mallory said before taking on Mount Everest in 1924.

For a successful assault, all components must mesh smoothly, and whichever members of the team wind up atop the summit, they and their teammates will recognize that they could not have done it alone.

Let's look at how change-readiness occurs. Marie, a middle manager in a typical organization, hears that top management has a new strategy for the company. But she doesn't understand why the company should change at all; her CEO regularly appears in the press, proudly announcing record profits. How do you persuade her of the inevitability and necessity of change? How do you create the necessary process?

People generally take risks—in the office or on the Himalayan slopes—for one of two reasons: they want to, or they have to. Either approach works.

Tenzing Norgay, who stood on the summit of Mount Everest with Sir Edmund Hillary in 1953, joined the expedition because he was inspired to climb the highest mountain in the world. But he might also have reached the summit if he'd been walking one day and found himself chased by an Abominable Snowman. He might even have done it faster.

In large organizations, some employees need to hear the Abominable Snowman thumping on their door before they'll lurch toward change. Others will be motivated to climb higher and higher, even when they already have a spectacular view, because they believe the view will be more breathtaking from higher up.

Which companies are recognized for the Breathtaking View approach—for their desire to continually challenge themselves to change, for their commitment to do better "because it's there"?

Consider Hewlett-Packard, the computer and printer maker that has been profitable for 50 years. Or Chaparral Steel, among the most profitable steel companies in the world and one of the few U.S. steel firms that remained profitable through the cyclical recession of the last decade. Or Honda, one of the most innovative and admired auto companies—the first Japanese firm to manufacture in the United States and other foreign markets, and the first to establish a distinct upmarket brand, the Acura.

Other such companies include General Electric, No. 1 or No. 2 in every business in which it operates; Toyota, the most consistently profitable auto company in the world; and Cemex of Mexico, the world's fourth largest and most profitable cement company.

These companies create their own challenges, raising their standards and squeezing their budgets long before their environment forces them to do so.

When a senior executive of Hewlett-Packard was asked why his company was so consistently successful, his answer revealed a great deal: "H-P is usually dissatisfied with itself." At Chaparral Steel, Gordon Forward, the CEO, similarly summarized the challenge he poses for his staff: "If it ain't broke—break it!" Honda turns to slogans such as "Something New from Everyone" or "Squeezing the Dry Towel."

 ## GROVE'S LAW

"Only the paranoid survive."
—*Andrew Grove, CEO of the Intel Corporation.*

All Breathtaking View companies share the same attitude: Never satisfied, never resting, never good enough. That's a pretty good attitude for an organization that wants to stay ahead in the twenty-first century.

The Abominable Snowman approach may work, but it's riskier. Impending doom can indeed concentrate the mind, but it limits options as well. Running away all the time is tiring; moving from one crisis to another is wearing and invites organizational burnout. The biggest risk, though, is that managers who take the Abominable Snowman approach end up trying to cheat: Convinced that change happens only during crisis, they invent a crisis.

There is a better way—a Middle Way.

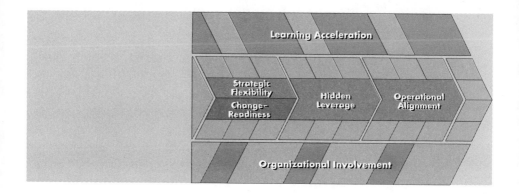

BECAUSE IT'S THERE

APPEALING TO PEOPLE

"Scaring people isn't the answer. You try to appeal to them. The more they understand why you want change, the easier it is to commit to it. And they must believe they can win. You have to define a goal line, so if they're successful, they have a chance to stop and say, 'Hey, this is a victory.' Celebration is crucial."
—*Lawrence Bossidy, CEO of Allied Signal.*

When there's no crisis, don't invent one. The better way is to convince people of the necessity for change by showing them the attractions of the specific change you're proposing. Remember management vision: Develop a vision that people want to become part of. If people are attracted to the vision, they'll buy the need for change.

Because you're trying simultaneously to tackle the first two change-readiness criteria—convincing people of the need to change, and convincing them of the appropriateness of a specific change—be prepared to put in double the effort.

And in contrast to crisis management, where the crisis provides an emotional push, managing for change-readiness requires that you create an emotional pull. You'll use these "emotional magnets" to attract the hearts and minds of people throughout the organization.

People respond to emotional magnets in two ways. Visions of wonderful possibilities pull us in: a sports team striving to win a championship, soldiers straining to break through enemy lines, employees cooperating to win a major contract. These positive visions contain a clear aspiration, evoke an inspirational response and contain enough practical details to be believable.

Horrible visions create magnets that are just as strong, pushing us away as far as we can get—but with a clearer picture of what awaits than the push of crisis management. A team's owner or manager can threaten trades, or send players down to minor leagues to be replaced by younger, hungrier athletes; a CEO can threaten layoffs.

These repulsing magnets, while powerful, are riskier to use than attracting magnets, because they are difficult to control and can have long-term side effects. The lack of control comes from the reaction they engender: You know that people will try to run away from the nasty vision, but you don't know where they will run to.

Such negative visions can also be debilitating. Fear acts as a corrosive. It's stressful and tiring, numbing. Long-term exposure destroys rather than builds, which is why "change through continued crisis" is not a valid long-term option. It's simply not sustainable.

■ THE MIDDLE WAY

Between the negative vision and the glowing positive one lies a Middle Way: a pragmatic combination of the two, using both poles of an emotional magnet.

Start with a positive vision that is as powerful as possible. Then use the negative to create dissatisfaction with the status quo, so that everyone wants to move away from the current reality.

But channel that dissatisfaction. A vision that creates frustration without showing a clear path to alleviating it will create a feeling of inadequacy that is almost as destructive as fear. Beware!

You can sometimes increase the strength of the dipole magnet by emphasizing the contrast between the positive and negative visions. This is what Jack Welch, the CEO, did at General Electric. The positive pole was strong: "We will be #1 or #2 in every business." The negative pole was the implied threat that any business that did not achieve "#1 or #2" would be sold.

Your goal is to underline the difference between the two poles.

■ CREATING A CASCADE

One powerful magnet can occasionally catalyze aligned change in large groups of people. Consider some of the world's major religions, started by a single individual and one intense emotional magnet.

But often an organization will not be able to create sufficient change using only a "supermagnet." So the positive vision needs to be reinforced by subsidiary magnets: detailed, complementary visions.

The development of subsidiary magnets is central to the roll-out of a Relativistic Strategy—a reflective, emergent, engaging process. At the team level, subsidiary magnets must be specific. Each team vision has to include a concrete goal so people will know when they've reached it. As with corporate visions, the best team visions include goals and suggestions of the means to achieving the goals.

Like corporate visions, the subsidiary magnets must be inspirational if they're to attract team members to do something differently—and maybe with a different spirit—to achieve their goals. It's not just about doing the same thing harder, with everyone running faster on parallel tracks. It's about attempting to move a huge rock. Financial goals alone are rarely adequate to create this kind of inspiration; supervisors or employees are hardly likely to be inspired every morning by the thought of increasing shareholder value for people they usually don't know.

Much more likely to succeed is a team vision that embodies Aspiration, Inspiration and Perspiration—the three components of the corporate vision. Like the individual battles fought in a military campaign, subsidiary magnets should embrace short-term goals that can be reached in 6 to 12 months. Winning the battle is a cause for celebration—a battalion taking a hill, planting a flag, celebrating and then moving on. Teams should celebrate each achievement.

 CHARACTERISTICS OF A TEAM VISION

1. Reflects Aspiration, Inspiration and Perspiration
2. Creates a sense of urgency
3. Has concrete goals, some achievable in 6 to 12 months
4. Has measurable and observable outcomes
5. Requires people to work outside normal organizational and mental boundaries
6. Provides occasions to celebrate achievements

With a corporate supermagnet and subsidiary team magnets in place, you need to address the remaining three criteria of change-readiness: How do you ensure people's commitment? How do you ensure they know what to do? And how do you ensure that "The System" doesn't fight them?

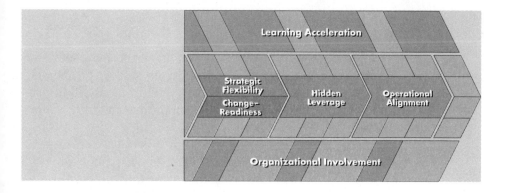

FORMING THE TEAM

 AN OLD CHINESE SAYING

"Tell me and I will forget. Show me and I may remember. Involve me and I will care."

The first stage of gaining commitment for an initiative is to consider who all the main participants are. Generally, there are four different kinds: Sponsors, Doers, Enablers and Supporters.

Sponsors, typically senior executives, don't need to be kept aware of all the details of plans and resources, but their support behind the scenes is essential and provides the team with the confidence that it can break through any logjams. For mold-breaking initiatives, the CEO is often the appropriate sponsor.

The Doers are the people who will have to incorporate change into their daily actions. To ensure their deep emotional involvement in the changes, they should be involved in the design of the change initiative.

The Enablers (and potential disablers) are the people who can authorize, or refuse to authorize, the use of resources—including the time the Doers need for the initiative to be a success. Enablers are typically the direct supervisors of Doers; they may also be union officers or managers of staff departments that control critical resources.

The Supporters are those whose help the team may need but who can probably continue to perform much as they did before. The accounting department, for instance, might be asked to provide information more frequently. Or, Supporters might be external suppliers.

One common mistake in change initiatives is to fail to recognize a key Sponsor, Doer, Enabler or Supporter. An even more common error is to go too far the other way and assume that the whole organization must be involved with the initiative. This invites a logistics nightmare and a drain on the firm's stretched resources.

 ## TOO MUCH PARTICIPATION

At one Latin American multinational, the general manager of a division launched a change program covering all of his many plants. Plant managers reported to a production director, who was therefore a key Enabler. But the general manager, following the advice of his consultants to be actively and visibly involved with major change, participated in every program meeting at each plant.

Unfortunately, the general manager's visible role diminished the role of the production director, who began to feel that he wasn't being acknowledged. Unintentionally, the production director became a disabler. To have some control, he began his own, small, parallel initiatives. And those diverted the time and attention of the people in the plants away from the major change initiative.

The logjam was broken by specifying the roles of the key players: The general manager was encouraged to step up to his role as a Sponsor, and to allow the production manager to take more responsibility—and get more credit—for the initiative, in the role of Enabler.

So concentrate on who the key players are, and which are Sponsors, Doers, Enablers or Supporters. Together, they probably make up a large enough group. Leave the rest of the organization alone, and it will be drawn in naturally.

And beware this trap:

Good managers know it's important to acknowledge people's contributions and not to brush them aside in the move for major change. They also know that an important way to acknowledge people is to give them responsibility. Too many managers thus assume they should involve in the initiative any important person who needs to be acknowledged.

That approach is often wrong. Just because people have done great things in the past does not make them ideal to help create the future. Quite the reverse: their achievements can wed them too much to the past.

When we conducted a large survey of firms that had undergone substantial change, one lesson the companies claimed to have learned was the need for CEOs to address the roles and performance of their senior teams far earlier than they had.

If you don't, you risk shackling the future.

 ## THE DRUCKER PERSPECTIVE

Peter Drucker, grand guru of management change, once gave this advice to a CEO unable to choose between selecting people according to performance and selecting them according to loyalty: Open new corporate offices, far better appointed than the present ones, and move all the very senior people into them, giving them fancy titles. In the old offices, retain only those managers who have the potential to lead change.

Having the senior people out of the way, doing peripheral things, will wind up costing far less than the status quo, because the firm will be able to move far faster.

(Alternatively, the CEO and his change-oriented managers can move out, leaving the rest behind, as Jack Smith did at General Motors soon after he took over as CEO.)

To achieve your goal of honoring what has been good in the past while making it easy to break out in new directions, you may find that you need to let some people go. You should do this, too, with honor.

But even if organizations find that a few people have to be let go to effect change, they are certain to find many more old practices that need to be done away with. And, surprisingly, disengaging practices can be even more difficult than disengaging people.

ENSURING ACKNOWLEDGEMENT THROUGH THE SEVEN STAGES OF MOVING ON

How can you decide what to keep and what to discard? As ever, the pragmatic path is the Middle Way: Keep the best of the old as a foundation, but let much of the old go to make room for the new. This approach allows an organization to keep producing short-term business results even as it redesigns itself to thrive in a changing environment.

SHEDDING OLD RULES

At the Santa Fe Institute in New Mexico, mathematicians and scientists in physics, chemistry, biology, economics and computer science look at the mechanisms and principles whereby organisms and other complex systems change and learn. One principle of survival they've observed is continuous shedding of operating rules that cease to be relevant because of changing environmental conditions.

They found that complex systems, whether biological organisms or computer systems, can hold only a small number of rules in operation at any time. So they must have an ability to shed old rules to make room for the new. Shedding becomes more complicated in systems involving human beings, because their sense of self-worth is often attached to many old rules.

First, you need to determine the characteristics of your new company. Then you need to take stock of how your company looks now and validate all the current practices against what you'll need in the future. You're bound to recognize a number of current practices that will fit, perhaps with a little modification. When you do, share the finding with other parts of the organization.

This not only preserves the sound practices, but it is a form of acknowledging and celebrating the successes of the past (as well as providing an opportunity to celebrate individuals).

Along the way, you'll occasionally be reminded of what wasn't quite so good about the good old days. And, above all, you'll get excited about the future because your personal vision will be tied up in the shared vision of the organization.

Characterizing, validating, recognizing, sharing, celebrating, letting go with honor, and then getting excited. This process has worked well in many firms—even old, tradition-bound firms.

Yet if you consider each of the seven stages in turn, you'll recognize the human face of change reflected in each of them (and you'll notice that in many ways the seven stages utterly contradict

THE SEVEN STAGES OF MOVING ON

1. **CHARACTERIZE** the organization of the future

2. **VALIDATE** existing practices against what's needed

3. **RECOGNIZE** existing practices that are suitable for the future

4. **SHARE** what you've found with the rest of the organization

5. **CELEBRATE** what will work and what has worked in the past

6. **LET GO WITH HONOR** practices that will hold the organization back

7. **GET EXCITED** about the future

some recommendations made in recent years by advocates of Rambo Reengineering).

Cemex, the Mexican cement giant, provides a study of how this process can work. Its management saw the company as very successful—witness their high profits and large market share. But they recognized that they might have to change because the world was evolving, with trade barriers lowered and competition increased.

But Cemex had a dilemma: How could it let go, with honor, practices that had served their time, while keeping people who had vested interests in those practices?

They followed the Seven Stages of Moving On. They decided they must determine what had made them so successful, to see whether it would remain valid. At each of 14 plants in Mexico, a team of managers characterized the type of organization they would have to be in the future.

Recognizing that people were their only appreciating asset, they asked what principles Cemex should adopt for organizing and developing its work force.

Then they asked how Cemex should manage production, maintenance and quality in the plants so that they would be world-class. To do this, they benchmarked manufacturing practices in their industry and others, not so much to set numerical goals as to help them visualize how a high-performing manufacturing operation would run.

Finally, they asked what type of management practices they would need.

Involving ever-increasing numbers of people in the plants, they validated what they were doing against what they would like to do. This participative exercise uncovered many practices that had contributed to the plants' performance—but that had not received recognition in the past. These practices were shared with all the other plants, giving credit to the originators and the practitioners.

Having celebrated the best practices, everyone found it far easier to let go of those practices that would become out of date, and to get excited about the future. Though some people were left worrying if their skills were up to the task.

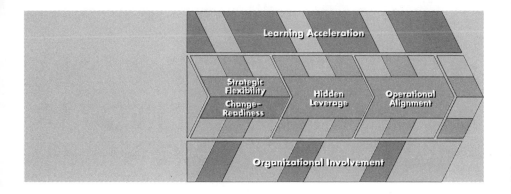

HONING
AND POLISHING

Transformational change involves a number of skills, and they are generally higher-level skills. So people may be excited and eager to change—but also worried.

What if they don't have the skills to do what's expected of them? They need to know what new things they may have to do, and to be reassured that they'll be helped to learn to do them.

Training, retraining and then retraining again has become an essential aspect of an organization's ability to change and to survive. Solectron, the Baldridge Award-winning assembler of printed circuit boards, estimates that as a result of the pace of change in technology, 20 percent of its engineers' knowledge becomes obsolete every year.

So every year Solectron employees, from entry-level workers to the chairman, spend an average of 110 hours in training, all during normal working hours. At Motorola, executives believe that in the coming business wars, the most crucial weapons will be responsiveness, adaptability and creativity. To hone those attributes, Motorola is developing what it calls "lifelong learning." By the year 2000, it proposes to quadruple the training it gives employees, from the current average level of 40 hours a year to almost four weeks' worth.

The benefits of training are apparent not only in the appreciation of the company's preparedness; they also improve the bottom line. Motorola calculates that every $1 it spends on training delivers $30 in productivity gains within three years. In five years, the company cut costs by $3.3 billion—not by shedding workers, but by training them to simplify processes and reduce waste. Sales per employee doubled, and profits increased 47 percent.

In 1993, Motorola spent 4.2 percent of payroll on training. General Electric spent even more—4.6 percent. Texas Instruments and Corning each spent 3.0 percent.

■ TWO PRINCIPLES OF TRAINING

Just because training *can* make all the difference in an ever-changing world does not mean that it *will* make that difference. Many organizations that spend a fortune on training never seem to get the full benefit.

Successful training in modern organizations should embody two universal principles: Just in Time and Task Aligned.

People should only be trained in something just before they will have a chance to apply it, and the thing that they are trained in should apply directly to a specific task that they need to accomplish. This leads directly to useful organizational learning and high performance.

Successful organizations use many ways to teach new concepts. Analytical concepts are generally best taught in classroom settings, while more tacit concepts, such as teamwork, are best acquired through experiential training. That can take several forms, some more successful than others.

Many organizations have experimented with games and shared experiences, both indoors—gazing-at-the-navel sensitivity sessions—and outdoors—in Outward Bound or similar programs. But participants have often had difficulty in transferring back to their business environment the concepts they acquired. As one top executive of a Fortune 100 company put it after returning from a dose of outdoor experiential training: "I don't want awareness training; I want to know how to do the damned thing."

So it's important to align the training as closely as possible to the environment in which the training will subsequently be applied—and to provide coaching afterward that will support people when they apply their training in earnest.

In managing for change-readiness, team training is particularly useful.

Teams take an actual problem to a training program, they work on solving it together, they commit to an action plan, and they become accountable for carrying it out. This appears to be the best way to ensure that effective organizational learning takes place. Companies including General Electric, Ameritech and AT&T use this approach to develop employee skills and to achieve breakthroughs.

■ RIGHT THINGS, WRONG WAY

Money spent on training can be wasted if the training isn't integrated with the cascade of magnets derived from the firm's vision, as an auto parts producer discovered. It set up a training institute that all employees were sent to, and the president of the firm personally reviewed the program's progress. In parallel to all this, employee involvement teams were set up all over the company to encourage employees to make improvements in their work areas. Task forces of managers were added later to focus on critical process improvement opportunities.

Yet, no one could see any great results from all this effort and investment. What was going wrong?

It turned out that the training, the teams and the tasks to be accomplished weren't connected tightly enough.

Employees went to the training programs in droves; they came together from many parts of the firm. This was seen as the only way to avoid straining any individual work center, and besides, it was thought to be a great opportunity for people from all over the firm to get to know each other, especially if their work never brought them together.

When the employees returned to work, however, they were pretty much on their own when it came to figuring out how to apply what they'd been taught to their real work. It was especially difficult if their immediate colleagues had not yet received training and didn't see things the same way, or if their immediate supervisors couldn't see the practical connection between what the trainee now knew and what the supervisor was under pressure to accomplish. In some cases, when workers came up with suggestions regarding the way work was planned and managed, they were told to mind their own business.

So, with a few exceptions, the training wasn't immediately applied—and if not immediately applied, it was all-too-often forgotten.

The teams of managers that were subsequently set up as task forces to obtain specific results never allowed themselves to learn the teamwork skills that the employee groups had been taught. That was largely because they believed that the skills taught had no real value because the employee teams had not produced any results. By denying themselves this very necessary training, most of the task forces accomplished little, for all the sound and fury they generated.

Top management, fortunately, did not lose faith in the value of training. When it recognized at last that the problem was caused by disconnections between the training, theteams and the tasks to be accomplished, they went back to first principles:

They developed a cascade of magnets from the vision and strategy of the firm. In parallel with that, they decided who needed to be involved in realizing the goals embedded in those magnets: Sponsors, Doers, Enablers and Supporters. That approach allowed for the creation of appropriate teams. Only then were the training requirements of the teams defined and scheduled depending on what they needed to learn and when they needed to learn it.

And the workers and managersfound themselves equipped with the skills they need to participate in change.

Of the five criteria for change-readiness, one remains to be discussed: The System, and Will It Support the Required Behavior? Chapter 3 is devoted to that.

SIGNPOSTS TO MANAGING FOR CHANGE-READINESS

Uncertain about your way? Let these guide you:

1. To be sufficiently change-ready, people need to find persuasive answers to five questions:
   - Is change necessary at all?
   - Is the proposed change appropriate?
   - Will they be acknowledged?
   - Will they have the skills required?
   - Will The System support the required changes?

2. In the best organizations—accelerating organizations—the desire to do better is a constant motivator, even when things are going well.

3. Magnets for change created by powerful aspirations are far better in the long term than pushes driven by fear.

4. Financial goals, by themselves, seldom inspire people.

5. The combination of dissatisfaction with the present and an aspiration for the future is a powerful impetus for change.

6. The supermagnet created by an overarching vision for change should be consolidated by a series of subsidiary magnets that engage people more specifically.

7. To propel change, a hierarchy of magnets must have concrete goals, create a sense of urgency, and suggest how the goals can be realized. In other words, they must have all three aspects of a good vision: Aspiration, Inspiration, and Perspiration.

8. In planning change initiatives, take account of four kinds of participants: Sponsors, Doers, Enablers, Supporters.

9. Honor those who have served well in the past, but ensure that the future is in the hands of those ready and able to change.

10. To make room for practices that will accelerate growth in the future, follow a seven-step process to let go of past practices that are now outdated:
    - Characterize the future organization
    - Validate existing practices against the future
    - Recognize current practices that are suitable for the future.
    - Share with the rest of the organization what has been found.
    - Celebrate what will work and what worked in the past.
    - Honor, but let go of, out-of-date practices.
    - Get excited about the future.

11. Training is most effective when it is aligned with the tasks that individuals have to carry out and is delivered just-in-time, as people need it.

12. Training plans should align *what* has to be accomplished with *how* to accomplish it and by *whom*.

Learning Acceleration

Strategic
Flexibility

Change–
Readiness

Hidden
Leverage

Operational
Alignment

Organizational Involvement

MANAGING FOR HIDDEN LEVERAGE

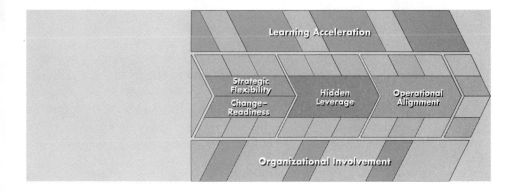

THE ILLUSION OF CONTROL

Compared with navigating a ship through open ocean at night, navigating an organization through change might seem a low-risk endeavor. If you fail to transform your organization, no one will perish at sea. But your organization may sink—and you with it—and a substantial proportion of your colleagues may find themselves beached.

If the rewards are great, the risks are too. So, it is essential to understand how your organization currently works—not just the formal structure, which you know, but what the unwritten rules are that drive it. In this part of the book, you'll learn how to uncover those rules and use that knowledge to avoid hidden dangers and to discover the points of greatest leverage for change.

You'll learn how to find the hidden logic that drives such rules. A vital tool in all this will be "systems thinking," and we'll see how it works through the five most common problems that change initiatives face.

When you analyze major change initiatives that have failed to achieve their original promise, 9 times out of 10 they still appear to make sense on paper. In other words, there's no problem on the surface.

That's much of the danger. As we navigate our corporate ships through a sea of change, we've only taken account of what we could see above the waterline—the formal, official ways our companies are supposed to operate (policies, procedures, organization structure, strategy, employee manuals). In other words, the "written rules."

Imagine that we're all running a global consumer products company. In the mid-1980s, our chief competitors step up their performance and we begin losing market share. The slide eventually extends to a fifth consecutive year.

So what do we do? First, we adopt Total Quality Management, and we trim back a little of our corporate fat—nothing dramatic, but enough to pep us up a bit. By the early 1990s, performance stabilizes and we have some breathing space. And we hear all the excitement about business process reengineering, so we decide to give it a go.

One area we're not happy with is product development. We want more exciting products, and we want them faster and at lower cost. We want to decentralize but remain coherent so we can grow internationally yet benefit from being one company.

We know that one key to achieving all that is for all the different functions and divisions to cooperate and communicate better. Remarkably, for once, people at all levels of our company agree with us: They agree with the need to change, they believe in the vision, they recognize that they all need to interact better than they do.

We have bottom-up enthusiasm; we have top-down support. And we know, from all those management texts we read in the 1980s, the importance of vision and leadership, so we put a lot of effort into those activities. We call our initiative "Pulling Together Into the Next Century."

We start ticking off the five change-readiness criteria: People agree with the need to change and there are strong emotional magnets pulling to our shared vision of change. So the first two are accounted for. We've agreed on all the practices that will hold us in good stead, everyone is excited, and we've got training in hand. So items three and four are accounted for.

To satisfy the fifth criterion for change-readiness, we decide we'll do whatever it takes to ensure that our new design fits with the rest of the business. How do we do this? We look at all the written rules. We'll consider just three of them here.

The first says: "To become a top manager, you must be well rounded . . . you need breadth of experience." That's marvelous, we conclude, just the sort of cross-business perspective that we're trying to encourage.

The second official policy says: "The best-performing managers get accelerated promotion from their boss," usually every two or three years. That's good, too, because people won't feel trapped waiting for their boss to move on, so they'll feel the benefits of striving for the new initiative.

The third written rule is hardly unique to our company: "The chief performance measure for managers is their profit and loss," so everyone will feel accountable.

Many other written rules seem to fit the change, too. With a platform like this, we convince ourselves that our product development initiative is going to be a tremendous success. Not only have we addressed the other four potential barriers to change, we've considered all the main policies and procedures of our company and verified that they are indeed aligned with our shared vision.

Now this is no surprise, but our company is not a make-believe one. This description was drawn from a real consumer products company. And reengineering failed—almost completely.

■ DESPITE ALL EFFORTS

Two years after all the initial enthusiasm, things were actually worse than before the change process started:

- Teamwork was poor, so lead times were abysmal and their costs were too high.
- There was no cooperation across the company, so decentralization risked getting out of control.
- There was chronic short-termism. No one was taking the strategic measures needed to grow internationally.
- No one would take any creative risk, so their products remained unimaginative—even boring.

The company's managers were bright and very ambitious. Everyone who had played a central role in the reengineering was highly professional. So why couldn't they see that their ship was about to run aground?

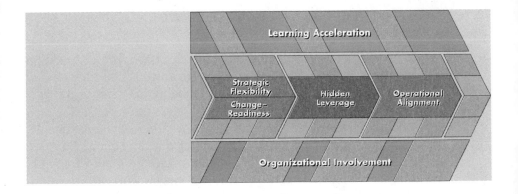

HIDDEN ICEBERGS

Why didn't the managers of the consumer products company see that their change initiative was about to run aground? Because they were looking only above the water line, focusing on the formal, written rules, the tip of the iceberg when it comes to organizational behavior.

Missing from—and essential to—their surveillance was what was going on below water level: what really drives the company day-to-day. The sensible ways to behave, for example, or the advice you'd give a friend on how to survive and thrive. These are the Unwritten Rules of the Game. They can differ dramatically from the formal rules, and far too many managers have misconceptions about them.

One is that the unwritten rules don't really matter: you can manage a business by only looking at the tip of the iceberg and focusing only on the written rules. Yet the formal policy of a company often promotes one thing, while what feels like the sensible way to behave can be the exact opposite.

Take the obvious example of teamwork. Almost every CEO these days is preaching teamwork and putting it into the Corporate Vision Statement. Yet all too often, when you look at the important rewards that employees get—not necessarily money, but career advancement or respect—you find that earning these requires you to stand out as an individual.

Too many CEOs offer a holiday in Hawaii or something equivalent for the individual in their company who stands out as the best team player. So all the ambitious high flyers go 'round thinking: "They want teamwork, I'll give 'em teamwork. When they look at a team, they'll see me standing out as being the best of the lot." Great teamwork.

Such a misalignment of teamwork is a rather obvious example, but still incredibly common. Many other disconnections between the goals of an accelerating organization and the goals of an individual are far less obvious—and far less easy to correct.

A second common misconception of managers is that acknowledging the unwritten rules is too "soft," too nebulous and intangible. After all, aren't unwritten rules something like "culture"? They're just there, with no particular logic behind them.

 ## IBM: THE BLINDNESS

Not so long ago, Louis Gerstner, the CEO of IBM, acknowledged that IBM's failure to capitalize on the move from mainframes to networked PCs was "the single most important mistake IBM has made." Why did they make such a major mistake, with so many very bright people in place?

One problem was the IBM culture—their unwritten rules, which reinforced the mindset of the past. To climb up in the company, you needed to impress your boss and colleagues. And they were impressed by mainframes. So why would anyone want to play around with personal computers? Everyone was making key decisions based on a reality that turned out to be an illusion.

When you fail to understand how unwritten rules are driving your company to behave, you risk becoming a dinosaur.

Of course unwritten rules *are* like culture; they are how culture can be defined. But that doesn't mean there's no logic to them. Indeed, after hundreds of analyses around the world, we've found that the unwritten rules are always completely logical.

The key implication is that if the behavioral barriers to change are caused by unwritten rules that are logical, then we can do something logical to remove the barriers—if we can uncover the logic.

Where the CEO preaches teamwork but everyone feels the pressure to stand out as individuals, the company needs to change the unwritten rules by rewarding teams. It could insist on developing shared team visions. It could use information systems to provide cross-functional teams with the right information to the right people at the right time and for the right reasons. And so on.

IBM: THE LIGHT

If Lou Gerstner had simply come in and tried to force change through despite the very strong IBM culture, he would have failed. Instead, he continues to put tremendous personal effort into trying to change the culture through a combination of shared vision that, in his words, "people need to feel in their gut," with the alignment of human resource policies, reward mechanisms, and organization structures.

Under Gerstner, IBM is profitable again. People feel a pressure to perform; fiefdoms are no longer tolerated; lead times have been halved.

Another common misconception among managers is the belief that they can take account of the unwritten rules intuitively. Good managers have always used intuition to take account of how people would behave. Why should now be any different?

The problem becomes clearer when you ask yourself where intuition comes from. The answer, of course, is from experience. And experience is based, obviously, on what happened in the past. So with the world changed and changing ever more quickly, intuition is something of a double-edged sword. On the one side, it allows you to cut through the complexity of change and make a decision. On the other, it can lead you to believe that you know how to react to a change, when in reality your learned response is outmoded, redundant or inappropriate.

In examining the logic behind the unwritten rules in organizations for seven years, we've been able to observe how they change. It takes only one shift in the economy, one shift in strategy, one reorganization, one change in government policy, the entrance of one new competitor or one reduction in the work force—and the unwritten rules of a business can be changed forever.

That is the problem of relying only on intuition: it's becoming too risky, even unprofessional.

The final misconception many managers have about unwritten rules is also the most disturbing. It is the belief that yes, there are unwritten rules, and maybe they're logical, but the key to achieving change is not to bother about the unwritten rules at all.

These misguided managers believe that if you're a real man (and nearly all the people holding this view are male), you can force through a change regardless of the unwritten rules, provided you push hard enough to make everyone follow as you leap off the cliff of change.

Think of these managers as macho lemmings; the species was much in evidence in the United States at the beginning of the 1990s. What a concept: Fire up your employees and then take a leap of faith, jumping into the waters below with the words: "Follow me, I see land ahead."

Except where a company was already in crisis, there's little documented evidence of that management approach ever working. After maybe a year or 18 months, employees sense that they're hitting a strong current caused by the unwritten rules, and it's flowing against them. Some people become cynical about the whole change initiative; others, who passionately believe in the new vision, put all their effort into trying to overcome the current. And soon they start to burn out. Eventually, they sink while still in sight of land.

It's a sad experience all around.

Tough but misguided management believed they could force through a change without overcoming conflicts between written and unwritten rules. Instead, they just forced the conflicts underground, where they festered. After a while, it was too late to avoid fundamental injury to the organization.

Don't misunderstand: The goal of business process reengineering is as valid today as it was at the beginning of the decade; it remains a very important management tool for achieving major performance improvement and sustaining it.

But not so the hard-line, sometimes brutal approach of Rambo Reengineering that too many companies have adopted. In fact, what these hardliners continue to advocate is tantamount to management malpractice. The real cost is not just financial, but tangible in the trauma, burnout and cynicism that fundamentally damages the resilience of the work force to subsequent change. Long term, these costs are potentially catastrophic.

 HOWEVER SURE YOU ARE . . .

"I beseech you, in the bowels of Christ, think it possible you may be mistaken."

A letter from Oliver Cromwell, 1650.

Because companies need to keep changing—and accelerating change—anything that damages the resilience of employees poisons the very lifeblood of the modern corporation.

Clearly, not everyone agrees. A number of macho managers, self-proclaimed gurus, and irresponsible consultants have a different view. Their approach encourages a lynch-mob mentality in which tough-minded leaders just "go out to do what needs to be done." If it weren't so dreadful, it would be pathetic.

Having seen the damage that they have inflicted, some such experts have made U-turns, leaving enormous skid marks behind them. Good. At least they've seen reason, and by whatever route they rejoin humanity is fine.

Having once been bitten, we now need be twice shy of any future suggestion that you can hammer change through an organization and its people. Outside consultants must work side by side with people from all levels of the company, and executives must do the same. Not because it's "nice" or "politically correct," but because otherwise they're doomed to failure. That's not touchy-feely softness at all. It's hard-headed pragmatism.

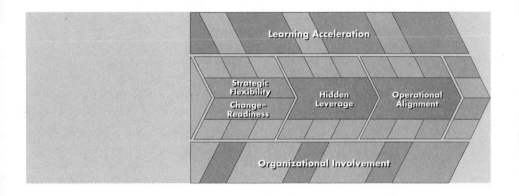

BELOW WATER LEVEL

It turns out to be far easier to uncover unwritten rules than anyone thought. The key is to apply a simple framework that acts as a miniature submarine and allows you to see below the waterline.

Remember that the view from a submarine offers close-up detail, but limited scope. You can explore a particular point in tremendous detail, but it would take far too long to explore everything.

So start with the business issues that are causing you pain. Focus. You don't want to uncover all the unwritten rules of your organization—only those that may be causing problems. To do this, you'll need to talk to people caught in the middle of unwritten rules—typically, middle managers—whether it be informally in the lunch room or in interviews.

Then, you structure your observations into three groupings: Motivators, Enablers and Triggers.

■ MOTIVATORS

Motivators are what is important to people, what motivates them. What makes them get up in the morning? What do they perceive as a reward? Just as important, what do they want to avoid? What do they perceive as a penalty?

In other words, you cluster together all the attracting and repulsing magnets that the interviewees respond to. These might include exciting work, respect, a sense of belonging, money, career advancement, or—and this is very common in a world of downsizings—being allowed to keep their jobs so they can continue paying the mortgage.

Motivators correspond to what is actually important to people, what they truly value. And so the grouping does not necessarily include such things as quality, even if the employees have been told how important it is to value quality. We've rarely found an interviewee who said he woke up on a Monday morning and thought: "Mmm, I feel like some . . . TQM today." Typically three to five Motivators drive behavior in an organization.

■ ENABLERS

Closely associated with what is important to your interviewees is who is important. These are the Enablers. Who can enable your interviewees to get what's important to them? Who can grant the reward or impose the penalty? You're not looking for who it's supposed to be, but who it is, because that represents the actual power structure of your company, in effect, the Unwritten Organization. Despite their absence from many official organizational charts, for example, key secretaries are often Enablers.

■ TRIGGERS

Triggers are how people get what's important to them: the conditions that lead an Enabler to grant a reward or impose a penalty. Triggers include all the perceived formal and informal performance measures.

Let's see how this framework of what-who-how helps us understand that troubled consumer products company by looking below the waterline.

 UNWRITTEN RULES REFERENCE

A detailed methodology of how to uncover the chains of logic behind unwritten rules and how to apply that knowledge to removing barriers is included in Peter Scott-Morgan's "The Unwritten Rules of the Game" (New York: McGraw-Hill, 1994).

What's the primary Motivator for people in the company? Remember how ambitious they all were. One key Motivator was career advancement.

How was this Motivator affected by the written rules? The first rule was "To become a top manager, you need broad experience." So the sensible way to proceed—the unwritten rule—was: "To get to the top, job-hop within the firm as fast as possible."

How about Enablers? Remember the second written rule: "The best-performing managers get accelerated promotion"—from their boss. So the key Enabler is the line boss. Now, even before our interviewee tells us any unwritten rules, we can almost predict what they'll be. What are the sensible ways to behave when only your boss can give you that thing you value most? Let's forgo the less-savory phrases that may spring to mind and simply phrase it as "Keep your boss happy."

Another rule is "Stand out from the crowd," so you'll be noticed as a top performer. If people submerge their egos and become genuine team players, they'll rightly worry that someone less modest will get promoted. So the critical behavior for promotion is to be seen—at least, when things are going well. The flip side is to "Avoid association with failure"; never let your boss see you fail.

Whether we approve or disapprove of some of these behaviors, and whether we consider them to be good or bad business practices, they're perfectly understandable, even logical. Working under such circumstances, we would all feel a strong pressure to conform to the logic of the unwritten rules—even if through great strength of character, or mule-like stubbornness, we acted differently.

What about Triggers? Remember the consumer product company's third written rule: "Managers are accountable for their profit and loss."

So the key performance measure that will persuade a boss to grant that coveted promotion is a manager's bottom line. How nice and quantitative, how conveniently nonsubjective, the boss will feel. Very understandable. But if we look for the unwritten rules, they're as logical and as predictable as all the others.

The first rule is "Protect your own turf." There are no rewards in this organization for helping to grow someone else's empire. In fact, there's something of a penalty, because then you will be spending less time on the activities that do bring rewards.

The second Trigger unwritten rule is "Watch your quarterlies." The CEO may talk about long-term vision and strategy, but people in the body of the organization know that if the financial performance of their area drops, the phone will start ringing.

Since there are never enough hours in the day, they know what feels most important, most immediate.

■ BUILDING CHAINS OF LOGIC

All these unwritten rules are not inherently good or bad. The question is: Are they appropriate or inappropriate to the changes the company is trying to make?

This company wanted to reengineer its product development process. So we need to investigate how the unwritten rules fit with the reengineering program.

With such unwritten rules as "Stand out from the crowd" and "Protect your own turf," teamwork is going to have an uphill struggle to begin with. Combine that with keeping happy a boss who wants to protect her own turf, and people will not be inclined to spend time working with other parts of the business.

So cross-functional cooperation and synergy have a double reinforcement working against them.

At the same time, job hopping and the focus on quarterly results will tend to encourage short-termism. No one will stay in the same place long enough to feel the benefit of doing anything truly strategic. If they did set in motion programs that brought benefits five to seven years out, they would not reap the benefits, nor would their successors. Only people they didn't even know would benefit.

Finally, why would people take any personal risk in an organization like this, when climbing the corporate ladder depends so much on continuing short-term personal success?

■ THE MISSING LINK

The unwritten rules are the missing link in our understanding. But knowledge of those rules, on its own, is not very helpful. We need not only to uncover important unwritten rules, but to understand how they are linked to the tip of the iceberg above the water level.

In other words, we need to see how the formal policies and the top management behaviors result in making the unwritten rules feel like sensible behavior in the first place. Then, we need to understand how the unwritten rules combine to create the apparently immovable barriers that can rip into the underbelly of our corporate ship and sink our change initiatives.

Only then can we discover the points of greatest leverage to break through the barriers to change.

But we have another problem. We need to see how one iceberg relates to another—which way the floes flow. And underwater surveillance will be of little help.

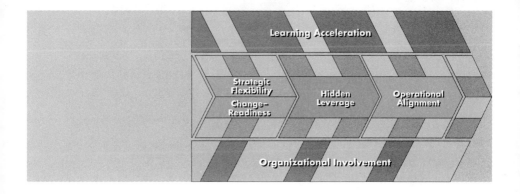

FLYING
ABOVE THE SHIP

To see how what you're doing fits into the greater scheme of things, it's necessary to do surveillance that provides an overview, rather than just details of potential hot spots. This broader approach is called "systems thinking."

Generally, people are not good at this. Indeed, there's not even a word in the English language that denotes the activity of "taking a systems view." Yet, we all can intuitively understand complex systems.

Why isn't systems thinking common in organizations?

If we're adept at seeing how apparently unrelated actions influence each other over time, why do we rarely apply this talent within our organizations? Because until we start looking for "the systems view," it's rarely apparent.

How many times do we blame one part of the organization when the real blame falls on the lack of alignment of the organization as a whole?

A common complaint in manufacturing companies, for example, is: "Production can't produce what R&D designed, and now Sales want something different anyway!" Probably it's no single department's fault, but rather an environment that doesn't allow them to communicate about the right subjects at the right time.

That is the first hurdle to overcome: The systemic problem can only be addressed when R&D, Production and Sales get around a table and manage to rise above a discussion that centers on finger-pointing. No single department can solve the problem on its own.

The next difficulty involves our perception of time, specifically how to take account of the delay between cause and effect.

A third hurdle is that the actions that systems thinking suggest may run counter to the knee-jerk responses that first spring to mind. An amateur gardener might be tempted to put down a powerful poison to clear his snail-infested garden. In so doing, he might destroy many valuable animals, including the snails, that feed on decaying vegetable matter. That would leave the garden infested with fungi. So, he might put down another poison to eliminate fungi, which might also eliminate the worms so essential to aerating the soil. The knee-jerk responses would, in the long term, create a barren wasteland.

The fourth problem that systems thinking must overcome is to avoid always starting from first principles. The solution is Pattern Recognition: Granted, all problems are different, but surely there must be common sequences of events within organizations? Not every pattern of related actions can be unique; we can learn something from experience.

About 10 years ago, Innovation Associates, a unit of Arthur D. Little, catalogued the most commonly observed patterns, which they called "archetypes." (The work was suggested by I.A.'s president, Charlie Kiefer, and carried out by Jennifer Kemeny, Michael Goodman and Peter Senge, the latter whom we now know for his work on the learning organization.)

The most useful aspect of the "archetypes" is that they suggest trends over time. In other words, they represent not static systems but dynamic ones, in which the relationships between different components are such that, over time, they lead to various classic end conditions. At one extreme, an archetype might point, for example, to a whole system unexpectedly crashing.

Knowing which archetype a system corresponds to can provide advanced warning of potential, even imminent, instability—and can also suggest leverage points for averting disaster.

■ THE LANGUAGE OF SYSTEMS THINKING

Two basic components combine to make all archetypes. The simpler of the two is what is known as a Reinforcing Loop, a grander name for the snowball effect: The larger the snowball, the faster it rolls down the hill, so the more snow it picks up, so the larger it becomes, and so the faster it rolls down the hill. . . .

In the business environment, an equivalent system dynamic would be a runaway best-seller of a product that takes off through word of mouth. The more people who have the product, the more happy customers there are; the more happy customers, the larger the number of people who'll talk about their new purchase to their friends; the more people who talk about the product, the more people who haven't bought one are exposed to it. . . .

Even at this level, we can see that every step in the chain is a potential weak link.

If anything adversely affects the quality of the products, customers will no longer be satisfied with their purchases. In fact, they could feel cheated and the same word-of-mouth process could destroy the boom almost overnight. If the product is personal or embarrassing to talk about, the virtuous spiral will never take off in the first place; if the benefits of the product are not easily explained, simply talking to friends won't motivate them to go out and buy it. And if outlets don't remain stocked with the product, people will not be able to buy it, however eager they are—a very common reason why sales slow.

Over the last few years, a way of easily describing systems has evolved that involves drawing a representation of a system following certain common conventions. Although there's not yet a universal standard and there are still some variances in symbols, we use a common nomenclature.

The snowballing product sales we've just considered could be represented graphically as follows:

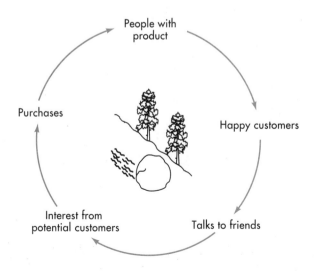

The classic behavior of Reinforcing Loops (often indicated by a snowball in the center but sometimes simply by the letter R) is that some performance measure, such as product sales, grows—or collapses—exponentially.

The second component found in many system dynamics is what is known as the Balancing Loop. Think of the dynamic of how you adjust the temperature of a shower: It's much too cold, so you increase the hot water; it's still not quite warm enough, so you open the hot a bit more; it's almost right so you open it more; now it's too hot, so you turn it back a bit. The target is "the perfect shower temperature."

The difference between the actual water temperature and the target is a gap, and the bigger the gap, the more you turn the hot tap. That, at least, is the theory.

But think about it. Is that what happens when you shower? All too often, particularly in an unfamiliar hotel room, the dynamic goes like this: The shower's much too cold, so you open the hot tap a lot, and as it warms up you step under the shower. But the water keeps getting warmer and warmer until it is too hot.

So with soap in your eyes, you grope for the hot water and turn it down. Nothing happens. Now you're practically being scalded, so you step out from under the water and turn the hot tap down a lot more. As the water becomes bearable, you step back under the shower, only to find that it's almost as cold as when you started. You turn the hot tap up a bit—but not as far as last time—and stoically wait until the shower becomes enjoyable again. Then it gets a little too hot, so you nudge the hot tap down and a little

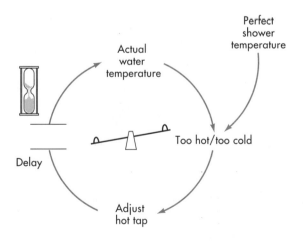

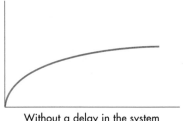

Without a delay in the system

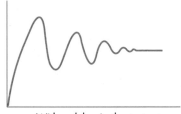

With a delay in the system

while later the temperature settles at the perfect value—just as you've run out of time for the shower.

What went wrong? Why didn't the neat Balancing Loop prove accurate? Because we forgot the problem of Time.

An unfamiliar shower is so difficult to control because when you adjust the hot tap, there's a delay between cause and effect. After passing through the tap, the water has to climb up a narrow pipe, force its way through a shower head, and finally fall on you—perhaps five seconds after you adjusted the tap.

The classic behavior of Balancing Loops is that some performance measure, such as water temperature, moves toward—and eventually settles on—the target. A standard symbol for a Balancing Loop is a see-saw, representing the oscillation that tends to occur as the system hunts for its target (you can also use the letter B). The presence or absence of a delay in the loop, commonly represented by two lines and an hourglass, makes a big difference to the observed behavior. If there is no delay, then the variable moves progressively closer to the target. If there is a delay, the variable oscillates on either side of the target and only eventually settles down.

Combining systems thinking with our Motivators-Enablers-Triggers framework offers a much more powerful tool for uncovering the best points of leverage than either tool does taken alone. While decades of systems thinking have provided us with archetypes of the most common recurring problem types, those archetypes—like all generalizations—suffer from not reflecting the full complexity of a real-life situation. They also provide little guidance on what specific solutions would best fit a given organization when it hits those problems.

The M-E-T framework allows us to focus on and uncover the detailed logic driving specific parts of a system dynamic. That can guide us to logical actions to remove those side effects and also offer a sense of the relative ease of alternative actions.

Together, these tools can uncover the chains of logic driving the unwritten rule sand the barriers to change that they form and also indicate what to leave alone. By focusing on the bare minimum we need to change, we'll disrupt the system less.

Until recently, many top managers seemed pretty good at sensing where the leverage points for change were. But, as all the change has become more and more turbulent, their instinct is starting to prove insufficient; that's why so many recent reengineerings haven't been a great success.

We'll continue by examining five of the many archetypes that researchers came up with—five we find particularly useful in revealing leverage points for change. The five are commonly referred to these days by cute names:

- Shifting the Burden
- Fixes That Backfire
- Accidental Adversaries
- Limits to Growth
- Tragedy of the Commons

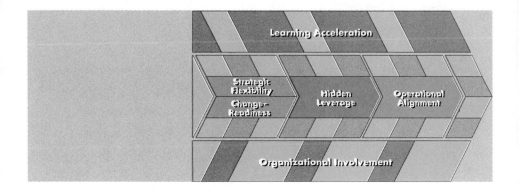

SHIFTING THE BURDEN

Remember our consumer products company, which excelled at slowly developing boring products? When the CEO caught wind of a particularly important new development, he decided to protect it from the stifling effects of the company at large.

Just as IBM did when it got around to developing a personal computer, the CEO set up a "skunk works," a self-contained unit that reported directly to him. In record time, the skunk works came up with the goods, and the new product did reasonably well in the marketplace. The strategy was deemed a success.

So the next priority development project was given the same treatment, and when it too appeared to be going well, another development was allowed to step outside the confines of business-as-usual.

Two years later, four skunk works were in operation. Each was performing well, and the rationale for setting them up in the first place had been more than vindicated—the remainder of the product development programs were performing worse than ever.

If we attempted to plot the attention being given by the company to improving its product development process, we would probably find that it was slowly diminishing over time.

These three simultaneous patterns—a quick fix increasing in frequency, a problem symptom oscillating but degrading overall and an increasing disinclination to take fundamental corrective action—are classic system behaviors of the archetype known as "Shifting the Burden."

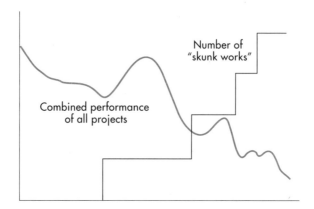

Because the quick fix (in this case, a skunk works) is easier to set up and shows results more quickly than attempts to take fundamental corrective action (such as overhauling the product development process), it feels like a sensible option. And the more often the quick fix works, the more it appears an efficient alternative to the drawn-out effort required to make fundamental changes. Indeed, the root cause of the original problem may be reinterpreted as having been the absence of the quick-fix solution.

But because the fundamental issues are not being addressed, overall performance gradually deteriorates. Often, because the benefits from the quick fix mask the steady decline in the rest of

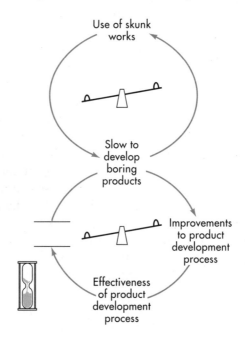

the organization, overall performance appears like a roller-coaster ride, alternating climbs and dips—but, overall, in decline.

What you need to determine now is why there seems to be a lack of interest in improving the overall product development process. The overview you now have is extremely useful, but the archetypes provide little guidance on what specific solutions would best fit a given organization when it hits those problems.

But combining the systems thinking view with Motivator-Enabler-Trigger analysis allows us to focus on, and uncover, the detailed logic driving specific parts of a system dynamic. It also offers a sense of the relative ease of alternative actions.

Recall now some of the specific details we found beneath the surface of this company:

- The individualistic reward system fights teamwork and, when reinforced by the command-and-control organization structure, tends to stifle any cross-functional cooperation.
- Chronic short-termism results from constant job hopping and a focus on quarterly results.
- No one takes any personal creative risk because so much depends on continued short-term personal performance.

So let's synthesize what we have. From the archetype, we know more and more skunk works are likely to emerge over time. And now we understand that the lack of interest in addressing the root problem is not simply a matter of the apparent efficiency of the skunk works. Instead, we can see, the reward and career progression policies are fighting people making the investment of their time to address the product development process.

The unwritten rules are such that even if a different product development process were magically put in place, it wouldn't work. The strong barriers to teamwork, cross-functional cooperation, longer-term planning and creative risk-taking all stand in the way.

Only once we understand what's going on beneath the surface do we realize that there are a couple of Reinforcing Loops in the system diagram that we missed on our first analysis.

The first loop originates from the action of using skunk works, which feeds the inadequacy of the product development process: The more that skunk works are used to isolate selected development teams, the more the old unwritten rules that lead to lack of cross-company cooperation and short-termism are reinforced. So

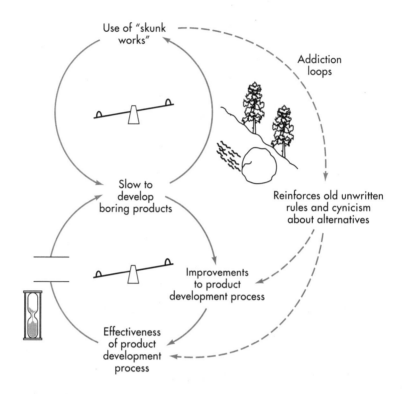

the more inadequately the existing product development process functions.

The second reinforcing loop also orginates from the action of using skunk works, but in this case, it undermines the very action of trying to improve the product development process: The more the old unwritten rules are reinforced, the less people feel able to take the long-term, company-wide view needed to address the product development process, and the more cynical they become that any alternative behaviors could ever take hold.

Both these loops are of the snowball variety, because the more that skunk works are used, the more they undermine the existing product development process and the ability of the organization to even address the product development process. So, the more that skunk works are used, the more they will need to be used. This is now no longer a question of choice. It has become an organizational addiction.

■ BREAKING THE HABIT

Attempting to go "cold turkey" from the addiction—dropping the skunk works—would be foolhardy. There's little evidence at this company to suggest that the product development process would improve, because the old unwritten rules would still act as barriers both to performance and to addressing the root causes of poor performance.

Instead, we need to work up the chains of logic we found to find what's really reinforcing the damaging side effects of poor teamwork, lack of intracompany cooperation, chronic short-termism and little creative risk.

The M-E-T framework really helps. Once we track back to what Motivators, Enablers or Triggers are causing the most damage, the framework itself guides us to the kinds of leverage points that we should consider, and in what order.

First, it's quick and also relatively painless to change Triggers. It's slower and can be a little painful changing Enablers, because there you're changing the power structure of your organization. But changing either Triggers or Enablers is far faster and less traumatic than trying to change what's important to people—in other words, trying to change the Motivators.

So, the pragmatic guideline is: Try to break through barriers primarily by changing Triggers, such as formal and informal performance measures, objectives, goals and milestone descriptions. A second choice would be to focus on realigning Enablers by changing such things as job descriptions, organization structures and information systems.

Only as a last resort should you consider changing noncore values. And core values, of course, should never be touched.

This is not how many executives handle such situations. Traditional approaches to addressing these sorts of behavioral problems have often focused on trying to change the Motivators, the shared values. Indeed, it's often the only thing traditional approaches can try to do, because they offer no chain of cause and effect to track back to what's really causing the problem.

So we've seen companies trying to "teach teamwork," "espouse quality," "encourage innovation" or "develop a customer orientation." Laudable though many of these goals are, all too often the companies in question were trying to remove the symptom—lack of teamwork, lack of quality, lack of innovation, lack of customer orientation—without changing the factors that made the symptom almost inevitable in the first place.

That's why so many improvement programs developed such a tarnished reputation. In implementing them, management was trying to push water uphill.

If, instead, they'd uncovered the logic behind their organization's unwritten rules, they would have understood the conflict with what they were trying to achieve. Once they'd understood the conflict, they could have explored how to eliminate it. Once they'd eliminated at least the worst of the conflict, they wouldn't have been pushing water uphill.

◼ A POSSIBLE SOLUTION

Following the guideline of Triggers, then Enablers, and Motivators as a last resort, you can sit down with your colleagues, pore over the system diagram and the M-E-T framework and hold a productive conversation about possible alternatives.

One avenue of inquiry might be to break through the ice at the point of the job-hopping unwritten rule. After all, people in the consumer products company are so obsessed with the short term because they're never around in one job long enough to feel the benefits of cooperation with other parts of the business.

Exploring this potential channel, your team might consider reducing job hopping by creating written rules that made promotions occur every five years, rather than every two or three.

On its own, that change wouldn't work, because a key Motivator for people is career progression. So, maybe managers could be rewarded for waiting by moving them two rungs up the ladder, rather than just one. In some organizations that have flattened considerably in the last few years, this option might not be valid; for many others, it remains a valid avenue for discussion.

Note that in this potential solution, the Motivator of career progression remains the same but is satisfied in a new way. If this change is made, the promotion decision shouldn't be made by the line boss, who might still be too narrow in focus, but rather by a senior mentor in another area of the company. So the Enabler would change.

And one thing the mentor would have to look for would be a track record of membership in teams that proved creative and willing to think longer term. So, the Trigger would change as well.

This was actually the solution adopted by the consumer products company in question.

And what happened? Within six months, the CEO was getting the behavior that he'd originally set out to achieve. Those changes to the written rules broke a logjam and released a stream of exciting new products.

ALTERNATIVE SOLUTIONS

What worked well for one company is not necessarily the solution for another. At a different company where job-hopping was recognized as a problem, the top executives decided to encourage managers to broaden themselves within their current jobs. Career advancement was made achievable within a given job, because it was made clear that one role of managers was to manage the interactions with other functions.

Here, too, the Motivator "Career Progression" remained the same, yet was satisfied in a new way.

Who was the Enabler that allowed managers to expand their roles this way? In fact, it wasn't a Who but a What: the information infrastructure that had recently been installed across the organization. Access to that system, and learning to use it in ways that would encourage those in other functions to interact on it, became critical. The Enabler changed from the line boss to the information system.

And what was the Trigger that set things in motion? The degree to which people were seen by their peers as bringing something to the party. If individuals used the network only for personal gain, their colleagues in other functions rapidly turned off. If people regularly offered information likely to be of help to their colleagues, over time they built up "credit" and would spontaneously receive valuable information themselves.

Those who built a reputation for being good corporate citizens served their own purposes as well—they gained the information that allowed them to manage cross-functional cooperation better, so their roles expanded. The Trigger changed.

In both these companies, the changes broke the addiction loops that were sucking the organization into a whirlpool of dysfunctional behavior. The companies were able to wean themselves off skunk works—over a couple of years. In parallel with pulling back from their addiction, they removed the original cause for it by changing their product development processes and bolstered those changes by aligning the most important invisible connections to Motivators, Enablers and Triggers.

And the unwritten rules that had been undermining attempts at change stopped feeling like "sensible ways to behave" and quietly disappeared.

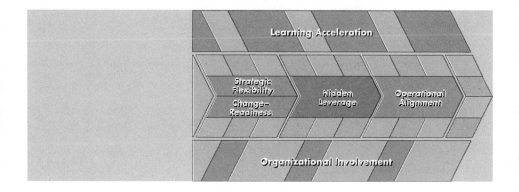

FIXES THAT BACKFIRE

To look at the next archetype, let's turn to another company. Although it has periods of significant growth, the growth doesn't tend to be sustainable, and worryingly, the overall trend is downward.

This fluctuating performance is following the classic pattern of an archetype known as "Fixes That Backfire." If quarterly results look as though they are going to be poor, top management encourages a Big Push from the whole company, and at least temporarily, that results in improved performance. But the diversion of everyone's energy to produce this short-term gain results in less time spent on fundamental improvements such as training and product development. Over time, the ability of the company to compete diminishes, and each Big Push becomes more and more difficult, requiring larger diversions of energy.

What is happening is that a quick fix Balancing Loop kicks off a Reinforcing Loop of delayed unintended consequences that gradually swamp the short-term benefits of the fix. Once again, though, understanding this system dynamic does not yield enough explanation of what's causing the situation in the first place, or much guidance on what to do to improve matters.

And once again, the M-E-T framework helps find the answers. You set up a workshop at which your colleagues are introduced to

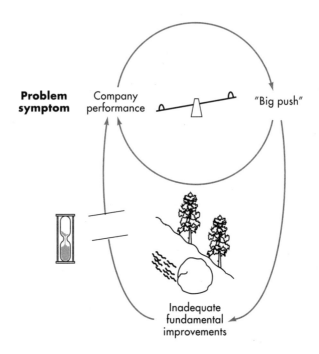

selected logic chains from the unwritten rules appraisal. The cause-and-effect chains should correspond to the two actions: Big Push and Inadequate Fundamental Improvements. It should be possible to see from the logic chains what the pressures are that create these two actions.

In this workshop, we don't need to work through the full M-E-T appraisal, because we're only really interested in the two logic strands relating to Inadequate Improvements and Big Pushes. And our appraisal finds that much of the stifling of Fundamental Improvements occurs in the body of the organization.

Let's look at the two most important Motivators for people in the body of this organization (important, that is, in terms of which takes precedence in a trade-off between doing something in order to satisfy one Motivator or the other). Motivator 1, the most important, is something to do with formal recognition, annual bonus (as much for the feeling of worth it conveys as for the cash), and job security. Motivator 2 is more about the feeling of doing a good job. The following diagram is read from right to left:

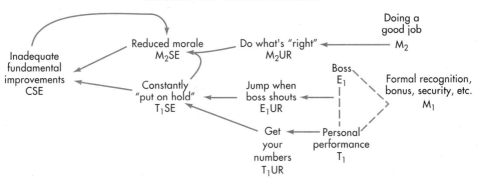

RULES FOR BODY OF ORGANIZATION

How does the M-E-T triangle relate to Motivator 1? It's pretty standard: The boss dictates the reward based on personal performance. So the most important Enabler is the boss and the most important Trigger is personal performance.

And under these circumstances, two unwritten rules naturally occur. One is "Jump when your boss shouts"; the other is "Get your numbers," because that's what the boss looks for.

When the boss shouts about falling numbers, it reinforces the focus on achieving numbers and quite naturally has the side effect of putting on hold those activities not directly related to short-term revenue generation. Constantly putting off worthwhile tasks such as training, as well as fundamental changes to how the company operates, ends up conflicting with the unwritten rule to "do what's right." This conflict results in a side effect of reduced morale.

Constantly putting important, though longer-term, activities on hold results in Inadequate Fundamental Improvements. Reduced morale has the same effect. Yet, the longer the Fundamental Improvements are delayed, the greater the reduction in morale of those wanting to do what's right, which further lessens the likelihood that the improvements will occur as the body of the organization spirals into a Reinforcing Loop of depression.

It seems clear enough. So why doesn't top management recognize what's happening? To find out, we need to look at their unwritten rules.

The top managers are driven most strongly by a desire for career advancement and power. Who can give them that? The CEO. What is she focused on? The quarterly results. So the top managers feel a strong pressure to take on a new job and then shine as quickly as possible, in order to demonstrate their prowess and suitability for still more power and advancement. They also feel a strong pressure to keep an eagle eye on current performance.

Those two unwritten rules combine to create a tendency to squeeze the last drop from the existing system. In other words, fundamental changes will take too long and won't bring benefits within the top managers' watch. A side effect is that top managers become fixated on the bottom line. All this is then amplified by the fact that people in the body of the organization will jump when their boss shouts. As a result, as soon as it looks as though quarterly results are going to be below plan, the signal goes out for a Big Push to bring things in on target, and the whole organization responds.

■ THE OPTIONS

As before, the most practical approach is to work back along the chains of logic to find the weakest links that, if broken, would correct the system dynamic. You can then discuss techniques to break the links.

Possible ways to break through might be:

- Have the CEO state corporate goals in terms of profitable growth and new products, training and so on.
- Set performance measures for selected individuals that go beyond sales targets. Include, for instance, product development targets.
- Measure top management using not just lagging indicators, such as profitability, but leading indicators. These measure what is expected to eventually translate into profits—product development and training, for example.
- Make more than just the boss responsible for bonuses and other forms of recognition. Add the product development leader, for instance.
- Encourage top managers to stick to their guns and panic less quickly. In other words, remind them to think of the long-term consequences. Have them internalize the system dynamic and M-E-T findings.

Conducting the unwritten rules appraisal using both the M-E-T framework and systems thinking provides greater guidance on the relative ease of effecting proposed changes. Conflicts derived from Motivators (such as "doing a good job" in conflict with "bonus and security") must not be attacked head-on, because that will only lead to corporate stress. Instead, the conflict must be removed by changing some factors that encourage behaviors that are means to an end, rather than ends in their own right.

That is, by changing Triggers and Enablers. Changes to Triggers (such as creating "performance appraisals of more than just sales targets") are likely to have the fastest impact. Changes to Enablers will take longer.

Combining M-E-T with systems thinking also helps avoid constructing an overly complex system dynamic in the first place.

A relatively small number of strong unwritten rules tend to dominate a company's behavior—a classic Pareto 80-20 distribution. So we don't need an academically precise, enormously complex mapping of a business.

Instead, adopt an archetype that best explains the overall behavior, then focus on the drivers of the relatively few unwritten rules that are reinforcing that dynamic in the first place. Although that will not remove all lesser conflicts from the system, it will be sufficient to effect change.

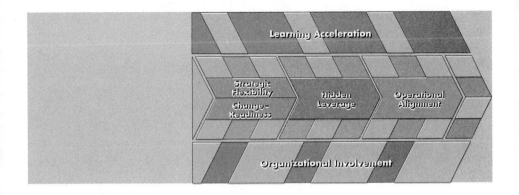

ACCIDENTAL
ADVERSARIES

Here's another archetype. Your organization has two divisions of roughly equal size: the Home market and Overseas. Each has a marketing department that reports to Corporate Marketing.

The Home division marketing is doing quite well, but Overseas is struggling. Despite a lot of support from Corporate over the last few years, its campaigns never seem to take off. What's more, despite the best of intentions from both sides, the relationship between Corporate and Overseas is deteriorating.

The pattern of behavior where the performance of two partners remains pretty constant (or perhaps declines) while their relationship becomes increasingly acrimonious is represented by a systems archetype known as "Accidental Adversaries."

At first glance it appears terribly complicated.

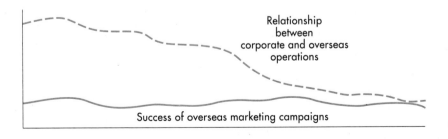

Relationship between corporate and overseas operations

Success of overseas marketing campaigns

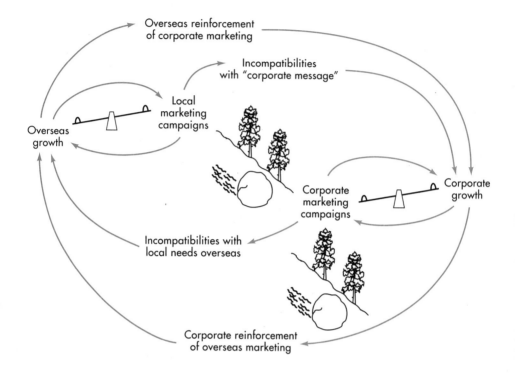

But what is rarely pointed out is that basically this archetype is made up of two Fixes That Backfire archetypes. The unintended side effect from a given fix impacts the other party.

The outer loop is a gently reinforcing one: The better Corporate does, the more it can reinforce Overseas marketing, which will help Overseas to grow, which will mean that Overseas can better reinforce Corporate marketing, which will mean that Corporate does better, and the better Corporate does . . .

That's the original Win-Win logic that the relationship starts with. If nothing got in its way, this virtuous circle would lead the Overseas division—and Corporate—to greater and greater success.

Unfortunately, each party unintentionally causes problems for the other. Corporate creates grand marketing campaigns for the whole company. They're great, but they inevitably suffer from not reflecting some local tastes that the Overseas division has to cater to. This causes problems for Overseas, which compensates by creating local marketing campaigns that highlight those aspects of the company most attractive to the local market. Those campaigns are great, too. But to varying degrees, they are incompatible with the corporate image that is supposed to be universal. And that causes problems for Corporate.

These two sets of "corrective actions" actually have the effect of creating a Reinforcing Loop in the center of the system that threatens to polarize both parties into a Them-Against-Us attitude of mutually destructive behavior.

Without the system archetype to guide us, you would not be forewarned of the dynamic built into the system—however things look now, they have the built-in tendency to get much worse. Indeed, in the early days of the relationship, everything would look rosy. Only later would the antagonism between the two parties begin to show, and even then the true cause of the antagonism might be too far away—on another continent—to observe clearly.

Before it's too late, Corporate and Overseas need to sit down, understand the system archetype they've gotten into, understand that it is a slippery slope, and above all understand where each side is coming from.

They need to agree on ground rules to resolve who the key Enablers really are, for at the moment Corporate thinks it is themselves, but Overseas does not. They also need to align Triggers. Right now, Corporate doesn't feel the need to worry about local Overseas needs, and the reverse is true as well.

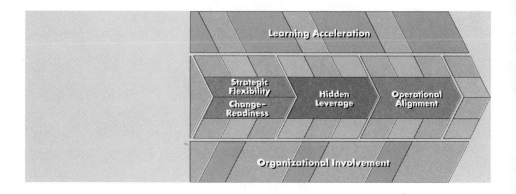

LIMITS TO GROWTH

You're part of a software sales division that's struggling harder and harder to maintain its excellent record of performance. For more than 100 quarters, it has had an unbroken stream of profits. But now, profits are leveling off and everything is creaking at the seams. The old administrative computer system is getting very long in the tooth. All the sales reps are suggesting that now is the time for a complete overhaul.

From a broad perspective, this system behavior appears to be a classic model of the "Limits to Growth" archetype. As profits rose, so the number of sales reps was increased, which fueled higher profits, and so on for almost 20 years. It was a comfortably Reinforcing Loop.

So what happened? Why did exponentially growing sales stop growing? Because they ran into a limit to their growth. In this

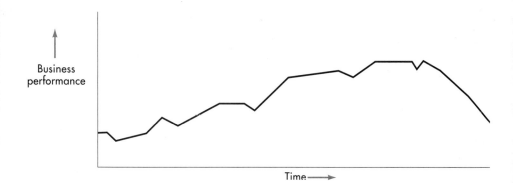

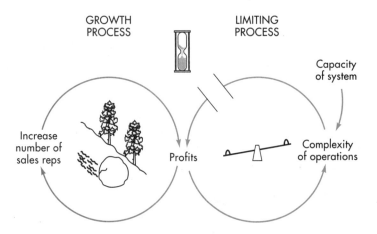

case, it's the capacity of the information systems as well as the human resources and training systems. In the short run, everyone can just work a bit harder to compensate. But eventually, the complexity of operations starts damping down the runaway growth of profits. It is a compensating Balancing Loop to the growth cycle.

The danger of this type of dynamic comes from the delay in the Balancing Loop. It introduces the same kind of effect as the lag of hot water in a shower: It encourages us to overshoot. At best, a Limits to Growth scenario suggests that, despite what would be expected simply by extrapolating from existing trends, in fact growth will soon level off—perhaps suddenly—as the limiting process kicks in after an unanticipated delay. At worst, the scenario alerts us to the possibility that instead of merely plateauing, our overshoot will so undermine our abilities that our capacity to generate profits will collapse. We'll become a classic boom and bust.

An M-E-T appraisal sheds a disconcerting light on the whole proceedings. It turns out the problem is far more insidious than it appeared from above. The whole division is permeated by a very consistent, potentially damaging set of unwritten rules. These rules lead to side effects of stagnation, suboptimization and stifled performance.

The stagnation shows itself in symptoms such as chronic risk aversion, cynicism about change—and the fact that management has not really done anything proactive in about 20 years. Why? Look at these unwritten rules.

UNWRITTEN RULES ENCOURAGING STAGNATION

For a middle manager: My bonus and career depends on delivering (ideally exceeding) my numbers. So, in general, I have to play safe.

For an upper manager: A substantial amount of my income is from the bonus that comes from exceeding plan. So don't let anyone screw it up.

For the Division President: I have three to five years to shine and move on. So, squeeze every last drop from the existing system.

These rules are reinforced by the fact that after more than 100 profitable quarters, pity the first person who breaks that run. And also because the stock options for upper and middle managers have two-year horizons, so where's the benefit of the medium term? For top and middle management, there appears to be only downside from the proposal, so the risk to the proposed systems overhaul is that nothing happens, or too little happens too late.

Suboptimization in this organization shows itself as "turfiness," little information shared across the business and very poor organizational learning. That's hardly surprising.

UNWRITTEN RULES ENCOURAGING SUBOPTIMIZATION

There are no rewards for growing someone else's empire. So concentrate on your own turf.

The only way I can reduce risk within my area is to maintain influence over my area. Keep your hands off!

The greater the number of people under you, the greater your power and prestige. So grow your own base.

We can never justify adding someone to staff overhead but can always justify adding someone to our own area. So do your own thing.

These unwritten rules are reinforced by the philosophical belief within the division that management practice is not to have staff overhead, and also the fact that job rotation across functions is rare because of different benefits packages. The risk of all this to the necessary systems overhaul comes in the form of a subtle but pervasive resistance to change: "We need to do it—but I don't."

And what about stifled performance? Throughout the division, it shows itself as a general cynicism about "the numbers." There's a lack of genuine control, and there's a tremendous amount of camouflage going on. The unwritten rules make this clear.

■ UNWRITTEN RULES ENCOURAGING STIFLED PERFORMANCE

You need to shine to improve your bonus and career, not simply achieve your targets. So low ball your estimates, then exceed them.

Everything's a game of negotiation.

We set incompatible targets for different groups, but they can't really compare them. So use numbers to stretch people rather than as measures.

As no one can really trust the numbers for planning purposes, and everyone's trying to exceed them anyway, we can get into terrible crunches. So don't expect a well-oiled machine.

You don't want to raise expectations, so hold back performance until the next financial period and maintain a healthy trend.

Because the corporate head office has become conditioned by this behavior in the division, it too plays by the same rules and expects the division to exceed targets. And the game continues in an ever-tightening spiral.

The risk to the overhaul is that even if the project ever gets going, there will be severe problems in the redesign discussions because everyone will treat them as a negotiating exercise.

And there's another concern: Each trend can't be taken in isolation. Stifled performance, combined with organizational stagnation, combined with institutionalized suboptimization, combined with heroic targets, combined with inescapable pressure to deliver leads to widespread and total B-U-R-N-O-U-T.

THE OPTIONS

Yes, of course, the information systems need to be completely overhauled. Probably all the other systems do as well, from recruitment and training to assessment and reward.

But some crucial measures need to be taken in order to break through the most dangerous hidden obstacles. In particular, it would be useful to address the preoccupation with quarterly performance, the risk aversion, the turfiness, the camouflage, the cynicism and the ambivalence about change among top management.

The fixation on quarterly performance might be tackled by negotiating with the head office details of short-term losses and longer-term improved performance. The overhaul itself would have to be engineered in order to ensure early wins, in order to help self-funding of the overhaul.

Risk aversion could be diminished by realigning bonuses and career advancement to the goals of the overhaul. Formal and informal reward mechanisms could be redesigned to encourage delivery on target rather than superpleasing, and to penalize hoarding for the next financial period.

Similarly, clear medium-term benefits should be constructed for those who would lose out during any reorganization. Otherwise turfiness will get in the way of creating an optimal structure for the division.

Finally, top managers could be encouraged to embrace change by realigning their personal rewards with the desired corporate goals, and by kicking off a visioning exercise—ideally, a short one—to create a supermagnet for the division (and for themselves). Then they could cascade magnets through the organization to help pull everyone onward and upward through the change.

And the division president could make unmistakeably clear top management's acceptance rather than avoidance of manageable risk, what the division's goals are—and his own public commitment to achieving the sustained benefits from the change.

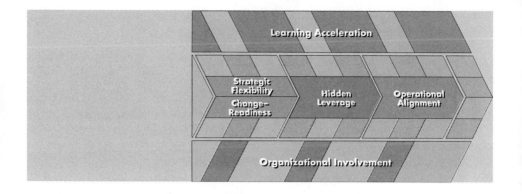

THE TRAGEDY OF THE COMMONS

Let's revisit that last scenario. But this time, you're in the head office, and so is the administrative system used by both the software and hardware sales divisions. It's the classic problem of the shoemaker's son going barefoot.

Two divisions have built up businesses acting as sales brokers for other people's computer hardware and software. The hardware sales division, by the way, was acquired 10 years ago, but the two sales forces have been kept separate owing to their radically different products. The corporate administrative system they use, however, has never been brought up to date.

And now there's vague cause for concern. The size of both sales forces has steadily been growing over the last decade, though recently it has plateaued. The individual sales reps are as active as ever; if anything, they're racing around more and more. Sales are all right, though nothing spectacular. But that's not the worry.

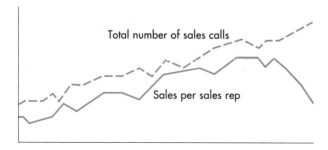

It's the average productivity of the sales reps that's the concern. Taken in total, more sales calls are being made than ever, but the average sales per rep have peaked. And now they're starting to drop steadily. Is it a temporary aberration?

We already know from the last scenario that there's an inherent problem with having the growing sales force using ancient administrative systems: the systems limit future growth.

And what happens when two divisions, each with a Limits to Growth dynamic, share the same limiting process? The compound system dynamic that results is far more unstable than either was alone. The reason comes back to time: The delay in a Balancing Loop always tends to catch us unawares. We overshoot because the feedback that we receive is out of date. And when two independent Reinforcing Loops are happily snowballing away, that same length of delay becomes doubly dangerous. By the time the feedback comes through, the combined effects of the snowballing loops is a massive overshoot.

This classic archetype goes by the rather poetic name "The Tragedy of the Commons." The metaphor is that if one shepherd lets a flock graze some pasture, everything tends to be all right; if many shepherds let their flocks graze on common land, overgrazing can occur so quickly that the signs aren't apparent in time and everybody suffers.

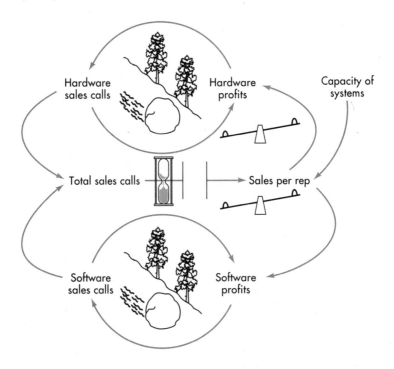

At our company, the situation is even worse than it appears from the archetype alone. Unwritten rules within each division compound the problems. These include: "We're independent, so we should do our own thing," "Keep quiet as you encroach on another division's turf—then apologize afterward" and "There's only a downside to helping another division, so look out for yourself." These are not team spirited, but that's not the problem. Rather, the problem is the side effect that arises as a result: Both the hardware and the software divisions have been trying to sell complete systems—of hardware and packaged software—to their clients, sometimes to the same customers. Neither left nor right hand is acknowledging that they are connected to the same torso. And the customers are getting fed up—and starting to go elsewhere.

Note the two new and important refinements to the system dynamic. First, the limit to growth is not just from the antiquated administrative systems, but also from a saturated market in which both divisions are chasing the same sales. Second, that market is diminished in size by the very action of trying to sell to it: The more uncoordinated sales calls made to a potential customer, the

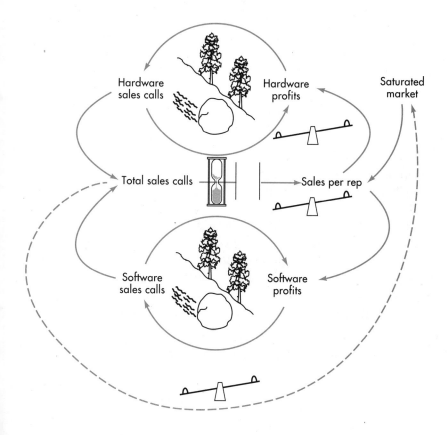

more likely the customer's staff is going to get fed up with the unprofessionalism they observe and take their business elsewhere.

This adds a new Balancing Loop to the system dynamic: The greater the number of sales calls, the more the market size diminishes. When this loop is present, a Tragedy of the Commons archetype becomes highly unstable and the results can be catastrophic.

What happens is that the massive overshoot of activity, brought on by two snowballing growth loops getting delayed feedback to slow their growth, combines with a massive reduction in potential to apply that activity. On the heels of wonderful growth, the system fails catastrophically. That is the true tragedy of this archetype.

■ THE OPTIONS

Now it's a question of survival. As soon as you and your colleagues recognize the archetype, you've got to act; remember that the feedback you're getting is massively delayed. Your team must act now.

Contact all your customers and institute damage control procedures. Put in place short-term mechanisms to ensure coordination between the two divisions; the procedures are bound to be bureaucratic, even draconian, but they're only temporary. Let everyone in the two divisions know what is happening—they need to feel the push from the powerful negative supermagnet. Then rapidly construct a positive supermagnet vision and have the two divisions flesh out strategy and tactics to achieve that vision. In the process, they'll create their own cascade of submagnets.

Urgently reengineer the two divisions—they need to be one— and replace that antediluvian administrative system. In parallel, address all the reasons you got so close to disaster and try to make sure it can never happen again.

Now, after all this time in the netherworld of managing for hidden leverage, we're ready for a new challenge.

In the next part, we'll tackle "Managing for operational alignment."

SIGNPOSTS TO MANAGING FOR HIDDEN LEVERAGE

For finding a safe course across the corporate seas, here are some buoys to mark the channel:

1. However clear "the written rules" of an organization, people's day-to-day behavior is driven by what they regard as the sensible way to act. These are the Unwritten Rules of the Game.

2. Unwritten rules are always logical, and you can neither rely on your intuition to understand them nor your power to ride roughshod over them. To try is to invite change-fatigue.

3. The goal of business process reengineering is valid—but an unduly hardline approach to reengineering is ultimately destructive.

4. To uncover the invisible connections to unwritten rules, use the M-E-T framework:

   • **M**otivators: What is important to people?

   • **E**nablers: Who can influence what's important to people?

   • **T**riggers: How can they go about getting it?

5. Uncovering the unwritten rules is merely a first step. You must find the invisible connections to those rules in order to hone in on the most damaging ones and change them.

6. Systems thinking helps address interrelated actions whose influence on each other is not apparent because of parochialism, delays, counter-intuitive repercussions and complexity.

7. The composition of any system's archetype is two types of loops (reinforcing and balancing) as well as delays.

8. The most useful system archetypes are commonly called:

   • Shifting the Burden
   • Fixes That Backfire
   • Accidental Adversaries
   • Limits to Growth
   • Tragedy of the Commons

9. The greatest dangers can come from not realizing how out of date some feedback may be. In unstable scenarios, this can cause a system to overshoot and collapse.

10. An organization should change the bare minimum required to achieve its desired goals: The less you change, the less you disrupt the system, and so the fewer problems you encounter.

11. Hidden systemic barriers to change—those unwritten rules—should be tackled by combining the M-E-T framework with systems thinking:

    • Look Around: What are the symptoms?
    • Look Above: Which archetype appears to fit best?
    • Look Below: What does the M-E-T framework reveal?
    • Decide: What links in the logic need to be altered?

12. The strongest systemic barriers to change should be addressed by realigning Triggers, then Enablers, and only as a last resort by addressing non-core Motivators.

13. Managing for hidden leverage links strategic flexibility and change-readiness with every other component of change.

Learning Acceleration

Strategic Flexibility

Change–Readiness

Hidden Leverage

Operational Alignment

Organizational Involvement

MANAGING FOR OPERATIONAL ALIGNMENT

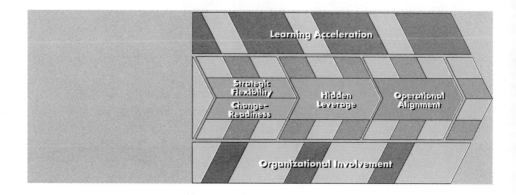

TRANSFORMING YOUR ORGANIZATION, DAY TO DAY

One of the world's mightiest corporations has been having a lot of problems in the last few years getting new products out as fast as its competitors, and in improving quality and productivity.

Yet it has one of the largest and best informed corporate staffs in its industry. The staff has more information about the latest management ideas, more industrial benchmarks and more comprehensive strategic plans than anyone else in their industry. But many employees describe what comes across as paralysis through analysis—the rubber never seems to hit the road and the firm's performance suffers as a result.

Managing for operational alignment, which we're going to focus on in this part of the book, is about weaving the insights from the other components of change into managing change day to day in a way that allows results to actually get delivered.

Implementing the new vision of an organization is never easy, even on a green-field site. Everyone has to share the vision, be willing to let go of their old mental models and be willing and able to work as part of a team. It's an impressive achievement when companies can create marvelously inspiring organizations, as General Motors did with its Saturn division.

But while the green-field approach is like building a new ship in a drydock, the challenge is far greater if you're trying to convert a sailing ship into a nuclear-powered cruiser, at sea, without jeopardizing the safety of passengers—and without delaying the voyage. And that's just what most organizational transformations are akin to these days.

Some consultants would have us believe that you can approach a transformation on a "start with a clean sheet of paper" basis. You can't; you have to go on serving customers and using assets productively. Organizations must continue to perform their existing activities well even as they try to transform themselves.

How can you run the day-to-day business as well as the change program? In principle, the answer is blindingly simple: You ensure that the mechanisms for running the organization are the same as the mechanisms for managing continuous change. Not only will you avoid being side-tracked, but you'll be prepared to cope with never-ending change.

To find the day-to-day mechanisms for managing continuous change, we need a clear model of change. One such model was proposed several decades ago by an organizational expert named Kurt Lewin. The Lewin model doesn't hold up very well for modern, continuous change, as we'll see, but it's still a reasonable starting point.

Lewin envisaged three stages to change: Unfreezing, Moving and Refreezing.

The first thing to recognize is that Lewin's model obviously applies only when an organization is happy to be frozen again, albeit in a radically different shape. For many organizations these days that would be a mistake; shortly after Refreezing, they are likely to have to go through another Unfreezing to make yet another change, and so on. In fact, we can see that Lewin's is a Newtonian model of change, clear in its mechanics but less helpful in a Relativistic world of constant flux.

Lewin also asserted that different management techniques were appropriate for Moving and for running the company day to day. In his view, Moving was an aberration, and after Refreezing, stability would return. These days, that is often not the case.

At one major corporation, for example, a senior executive stirred up his company to embark on a major change program, exhorting: "Do or Die" and "Everyone on Board."

But soon, the change team he'd set up could hardly get any executives to attend to the change-related activities that everyone had agreed were important. Secretaries explained that the executives were too busy with other more important matters. The change team reminded the executives of the new slogan that the executives themselves had devised: "Improving the Rate of Improvement is Management Job Number One"—a pretty reasonable description of what the job of senior managers should be in an Accelerating Organization.

So what were these more important matters that were getting a higher priority, the change team asked?

"Well, we've got to continue running the business, don't we," came the executives' indignant response.

Much more appropriate is a change process that embodies the principles by which the organization will operate in the future. And this ought to start from Day One.

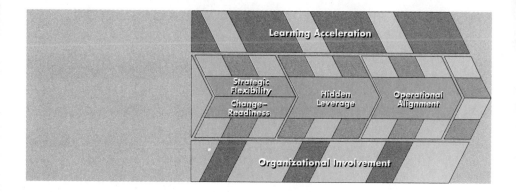

PREPARING TO JUGGLE

To build and retain the means for continuously redesigning and changing itself, an organization needs two components. One is semipermanent structures, such as major business processes; the other is change mechanisms, typically improvement task forces, that work across the structures.

When this structure is achieved properly, the change mechanisms remain in place even after organizational transformation is achieved, so the organization can continue to keep change.

■ ALIGNED CHANGE

To maintain operational alignment during change, the change mechanisms have to embrace three components. These are the design of business processes, the skills and motivation of people and the quality of the resources deployed. These three components are closely connected, and there's considerable evidence that aligning them has as much, if not more, impact on operational ability than the quality of any one of them.

In 1991, with The Economist Intelligence Unit, we conducted a worldwide study of manufacturing plants in several industries. Plants that had integrated Processes, People and Resources most closely not only had the best performance but also the best rate of improvement of performance. That finding was later confirmed by a comparison of 12 plants within a single corporation—the ones that improved fastest had the best balance. So, above all, operational change mechanisms have to ensure balance between processes, resources and people.

 ## IGNORING THE CONNECTIONS

Improving each element of a system separately while ignoring the connections among them is never as effective as improving the whole system.

One successful truck manufacturer in the United States had rested on its laurels too long, but it was determined to leapfrog the competition and make up for lost time. It ordered up a world class manufacturing facility. Engineering, Industrial Engineering and Personnel were charged, respectively, with designing the best resources, processes and people practices.

Engineering designed and installed one of the most advanced automated production facilities in the industry, including an automated materials storage and retrieval system. Industrial Engineering laid out a just-in-time manufacturing process. And Personnel, conceiving of a team-based plant with multiskilled operators sharing each other's work, recommended that the plant be installed in the South, away from union strongholds (although this also meant away from skilled labor).

Yet the plant did not produce a single complete truck for one year after it was commissioned. When the materials-handling system developed snags, the operators were too inexperienced to fix it; the just-in-time system left no margin for error or delay. Incomplete trucks were sent on to dealers to be finished, which affected both cost and quality. The company's change mechanisms were simply not in harmony. Eventually, the company sank financially and was taken over.

To achieve that harmony and balance, you have to work at three levels:

First, you have to tackle day-to-day burning issues—customer problems, equipment failures and local improvements at the operating procedure level. This tends to be a combination of addressing the consequences of things gone wrong and of unexpected events.

Second, you need to set up teams to address all the processes that cry out for improvement—including, but not limited to, customer management, supply management and product development. Addressing these issues should eventually reduce the amount of fire-fighting that's needed. Indeed, considering the root causes of recurring burning issues is the start of any process review.

Third, you need to set up teams to tackle improvements to the underlying infrastructure—information systems, training, performance appraisal—in order to facilitate the improvements in processes.

And, of course, during all this, everyone must remain responsive to changes made not just by competitors, customers and suppliers, but by colleagues.

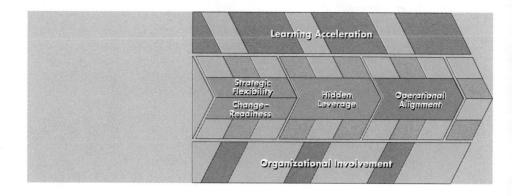

PICKING UP
THE BALLS

Most managers love action. But it's all too easy for a manager to become an efficient tube between an In tray and an Out tray, moving things faster and faster between them without noticing how the same types of problems keep reappearing. Many management meetings are run like the tube between In and Out: Items on the agenda are dealt with efficiently, one by one, but with more of a focus on this bailing water than on improving the fundamental performance of the corporate ship.

 ## RUNNING TO STAND STILL

The manager of a paper-making plant was anxious about the net effect of all the actions he and his staff had taken in response to problems. So, with the assistance of consultants, the manager and his team tracked 420 actions they had taken and found that 397 had no effect—or a deleterious effect. And responding to the disruptions that the managers had created resulted in further disruptions that required more interventions. The plant managers were like hamsters on exercise wheels—they didn't make any progress.

Operations managers in particular are under great pressure to meet closer deadlines, manage within tighter budgets and provide ever-better service to customers. Their calendars, their In trays and boxes for voice messages and e-mail overflow with "to do's." And it's in this context that they need to juggle operational change mechanisms.

Of course, a host of tools and techniques are available to analyze and redesign organizations and work processes. The Quality movement, Operations Research, Organization Development and other schools of management thinking have all helped fill the tool box. From the point of view of managing for operational alignment, it's not the lack of tools and techniques that prevents many organizations from achieving their desired transformation—it's the way in which the tools and techniques are used.

Operational change is about switching off the old ways of doing things and switching on the new. But those switches have to occur in the minds of people and in their day-to-day actions. That's why those same people need to be involved in the analysis and design of operational change, so that they discover and own the solutions. Only then will they be active agents of change rather than passive participants; it's not enough for a staff department or a consultant to apply the tools and techniques and then try to sell the results to others.

If an organization is to accelerate its learning, it needs a number of improvement teams that can master these techniques. Think of it as juggling three balls:

First Ball: Give one group responsibility for aligning overall specifications and guidelines for every improvement team.

Second Ball: Set up a multifunctional team for each major improvement task, initially at the process level, then at the infrastructural level.

Third Ball: Institute a formal integration process to ensure alignment between different team solutions and to compensate for changes.

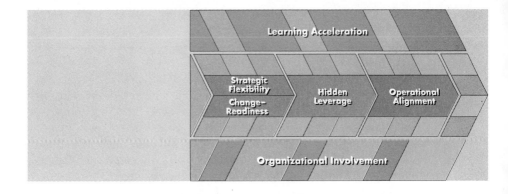

THE FIRST BALL

To align improvement teams, you first need to understand what it is that all the teams are to accomplish. That will also suggest how to manage tradeoffs between different goals.

A practical way to do this is to set up a Coordinated Design Group, which should include all the key players who will have to do or change something to implement the overall change that's envisaged. These are the Enablers; each member of the group may come armed with inspirational goals—a magnet consistent with the supermagnet of the vision and strategy.

At a company wanting to build a financial cushion against an expected market downturn, for instance, one group might have decided that its goal was to help build the cushion by manufacturing 6,000 products in 1996. Another group's goal might be to reduce equipment downtime by half through improved maintenance. These goals become magnets when the group feels they are worthwhile and feels inspired to stretch itself to achieve them.

An alternative approach is for the coordinated design group to define individual team goals together. One advantage is that it becomes easier to ensure that the goals are consistent and aligned. The disadvantage is that the goals will then have to be "told" or "sold" to the teams and may thus cease to have the pull of magnets for the teams.

However the initial magnets are derived, the coordinated design group has to consider how the different magnets are likely to affect each other. To do this, it has to think about the overall system and its interrelated components, relying on systems thinking and the M-E-T framework.

BEST OF BOTH WORLDS

Cemex wanted to become the Toyota of its industry, developing an ability to improve operating performance faster than any competitor. Management thought a leverage point for this was rapid improvement in the growth of the abilities of individuals and semi-autonomous teams. A key requirement on the People side, therefore, was to enable job enrichment and multiskilling.

Another leverage point for operating performance improvement was the uptime of the kilns and other major equipment, because cement production is capital intensive and interruptions in production are very costly. Maintenance skills are important, and specialization seemed an obvious answer.

This created a head-on conflict between the ideas of job enrichment and specialized maintenance. The group responsible for ensuring a coordinated transformation recognized the potential tradeoff and came up with a solution that met both requirements: Every multiskilled team contained a highly skilled maintenance person who could deal with critical problems as they arose and coach other teams members the rest of the time.

In fact, the coordinated design group at Cemex determined that it could view the key components of the system as an interaction between several social and technical systems, the principal ones being Human Resources, Production and Maintenance. The group decided what the key characteristics of this socio-technical system would need to be to create a high-performing, accelerating organization. Some characteristics they sought in the HR systems were that training should be provided on a just-in-time and task-aligned basis and that salary be skill- and performance-based. For the production system, essential characteristics included pull-based scheduling and work teams that dealt directly with customers. The overall specifications for the change, and the requirements of each component, were then used as a reference by all the improvement teams—even though each had its own responsibilities and created its own magnets within the overall guidelines agreed to by the coordinated design group.

Teams creating their own extra goals is typical—and desirable. For instance, the team working on manufacturing 6,000 products in 1996 might create additional goals to help pull members toward that target (as long as those extra magnets do not create potential conflicts with other groups).

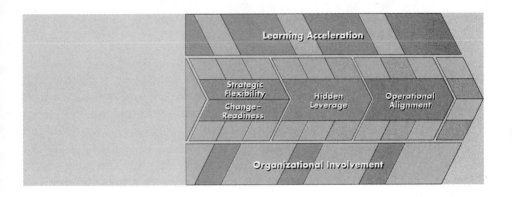

THE SECOND BALL

In order to ensure the alignment of changes, you need to set up improvement teams. Often this only happens after the coordinated design team has come up with overall guidelines.

It makes a tremendous difference if you bring into every change team people who among them can represent any perspective that is likely to prove relevant. This typically means bringing together representatives from the different functions of the organization.

Multifunctional representation helps in three ways.

 ## TEAMS AT HONDA

Generally recognized as an accelerating organization, Honda insists that any initiative of significance be entrusted to an "S-E-D" team (S for Sales, E for Engineering, D for Development). The balance of team members may vary depending on the size and thrust of the initiative, but all three disciplines will always be represented.

First, the presence of all the functions speeds up team decisions whenever it's important to reflect a number of perspectives on the organization. In particular, this approach makes it easy to combine broad systems views and realistic M-E-T views and then return to the decision or action at hand.

Second, some aspects of knowledge are "tacit"—in other words, they're not readily expressed but can be communicated through social, face-to-face interaction. Tacit knowledge in a team might range from the skill of a craftsman to the "instinct" of an experienced manager. This kind of knowledge has, by definition, not yet been codified and made explicit, and perhaps never can be, so the only way to share it is by working together on a shared problem. Very often, it's tacit knowledge that provides the real insight that distinguishes a great solution from a pedestrian, though workable, one.

Third, multifunctional teams benefit from sharing wider perspectives, which helps grow the ability of team members to manage for hidden leverage. More rounded managers are developed, which in turn gives the organization a better ability to manage complex systems.

It's unlikely that an organization will want to introduce a large number of improvement teams in one go. Better to phase them in, following this sequence of the kinds of improvements that teams need to tackle: operational, process, infrastructural.

Operational teams addressing day-to-day problems will probably be at work before the coordinated design group first meets. However, as a result of deciding the overall specifications for change, the group might decide to address some burning issues in order to provide more time for tackling fundamental issues. Imminent equipment failure, for example, might require urgent attention to tide things over until the maintenance process is improved to meet the goal of halving downtime.

Most first-wave teams that the coordinated design group starts will be focused on improving processes. When the group looks at the unwritten rules driving the business, it may then choose to immediately set up additional teams to tackle those issues, should it find obvious infrastructural problems in such areas as information systems or performance appraisal.

But often it is not clear what the best solutions to the infrastructural issues are, until the needs of the processes that the infrastructure has to support have been understood. As the various improvement teams refine their magnets and begin working toward their goals, the requirements for infrastructural changes begin to be defined.

When this happens it will be natural for the coordinated design group to start a new team, probably made up of experts on the infrastructural issue together with selected members of the teams that hit the infrastructural problem in the first place.

Of course, in order to sense the need to launch a new team, the coordinated design group needs to remain alert to integration issues. That's the third ball that needs to be juggled.

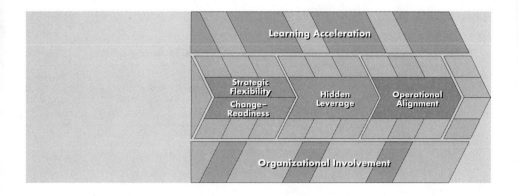

THE THIRD BALL

Let's assume you now have overall specifications and guidelines jointly developed by the key players who have to design and implement pieces of the solution: the coordinated design group. And you have multifunctional teams to ensure integration within each of the components.

But any slight change by one team may require other teams to review and adjust their plans—a commonplace of organizational transformation. So teams need a mechanism to integrate everything. To do that, they must jointly determine what is going on and how everything ties together. We call these "Integration Meetings."

The leaders of all the improvement teams should arrange to meet periodically (maybe every day, certainly every week) to discuss integration issues. Or, in fact, this group of leaders could be the coordinated design group itself, which tends to make integration even easier. Either way, it helps to have the overall specifications and principles agreed to by the coordinated design group displayed on the walls to remind everyone what they are. It also helps to stick to the wall a chart with the names of every change initiative across both the top and the side. This is the Integration Matrix.

The purpose of the matrix is to record in each box the requirement that a given initiative has on another. Let's say one magnet is High Impact Training and another is Downtime by Half. Inevitably, as the team struggling to reduce downtime progresses, it will identify requirements for the team addressing Training. This

Example of integration chart for manufacturing firm

Submagnets	6 by '96	Down-time by half	Double in 2	High Involvement	High Impact	What's where, when-ever
Six by '96 Manufacture 6,000 products in 1996, taking advantage of remaining market window to build financial cushion.			Production will be more difficult if flexibility is needed for customer service			
Downtime by half Reduce equipment down-town by half, through improved maintenance, to enable more production time and better asset utilization.					If we improve maintenance we will need skills upgrades for many employees	
Double with our best buddy in two Double share of business (of a chosen customer) by the time next recession hits, to be secure as most preferred supplier.	To improve customer service we will need greater flexibility in production					To improve customer service we will need on-line order status information
High Involvement communications Create a process/ infrastructure for more open communication between all levels to increase involvement in change process.						
High Impact training Create a system for just-in-time, task-aligned training to support achievement of the cascade of magnets.						
What's where, whenever Overhaul information technology systems to inform people on status of orders and production whenever they need it to achieve their magnets.					Change in I.T. systems needs just-in-time training for many people	

interdependency needs to be discussed, and the proposed resolution needs to be noted in the box where the two intersect. At the next Integration Meeting, the group can confirm that progress is being made on all existing items, as well as add any new items.

Using the integration matrix over many regular meetings, the integration team can see patterns emerge: trends of problems and needs that can give insights into the system dynamics of the organization. Systems thinking archetypes can then help the team quickly recognize classes of problems that it can explore more closely, using the M-E-T framework. The integration matrix also highlights when teams are running into demand crunches and may temporarily need more resources from teams that are themselves waiting for inputs from the overloaded teams.

The matrix is a way to convert systems thinking into systems action. It enables a team to act upon a detailed understanding of components of the organization in a systemic way and to see the systemic connections as the change proceeds. It's a framework for seeing connections between short-term and long-term requirements and so addressing both adequately.

A US auto parts producer had to urgently overhaul its two largest manufacturing plants to retain its major customers and avert plant closures. It undertook radical changes to its key business processes—production, supply management, maintenance, product introduction and planning—and to its equipment and to its organization—team design, de-layering, training and wage structure.

All the changes were closely interrelated, so Plant A decided to juggle the three balls: coordinated design group, multifunctional teams and integration process. Plant B adopted the first two but decided against the integration process; it wanted to stay with a more traditional management-by-objectives approach, in which once the objectives, resources and constraints were clearly specified, the managers responsible were held solely accountable. Of course, the thinking went, the managers could always ask for help if they couldn't cope. But what managers would admit to that?

At both plants, improvements were noted. But Plant A improved much faster and at a rate that surprised top management. And teamwork at Plant A was far better than at Plant B within a few months, even though it was worse when the overhauls started. That helped accelerate improvements still further.

The integration team process enabled Telco, an Indian truck company faced by an onslaught of Japanese competitors, to develop a new model of truck in only 18 months from conception to commercial launch—less than half the time it took anyone else in the industry worldwide. They called it Project Jupiter, and they pulled it off. Many parallel initiatives were integrated: not just the design and development of the truck itself, but also a new approach to machining technology using in-line machining centers, a new way to produce sheet-metal panels to reduce development time and a program for developing highly skilled and versatile master craftsmen.

Most importantly, Telco used the integration matrix to indicate when to move resources back and forth whenever teams on the critical path began to feel the strain.

New information technologies such as groupware now enable teams to meet frequently without having to get together in the same room or even to rely on a conference call. The integration process and matrix serve as well to organize electronic meetings as they do face-to-face meetings.

In some quarters, we've noticed a temptation to describe change teams as a sort of symphony orchestra. That doesn't ring true to us, because each individual does not have a specific score to follow, and there's no single conductor helping everyone keep time.

It's more useful to think of change as a journey into the largely unknown. The change teams are like explorers, or pioneers, shaping their own paths—or creating their own variations, on the fly, of a broadly known musical theme. But large-scale corporate change may also have to respond to the inspired participation by the audience—a customer, supplier or shareholder who decides to toot along, as well.

BE TRUE TO YOURSELF

"If you can see your path laid out before you step by step—then it's not your path. Your own path you make with every step you take. That's your path."
—*Joseph Campbell, poet.*

The level of decentralized self-regulating integration that's needed is difficult to achieve, and we've seen it only when organizations followed the three steps of coordinated design, cross-functional teams and an integration process. But when it does work, this self-aligned teamwork produces people jointly playing in harmony around a previously composed and shared melody.

When we revisited auto parts Plant A a few years after it overtook its sibling plant and Telco a few years after its phenomenal success at devising and executing a new approach to product development, we noticed something very interesting: In both cases, the integration process with its regularly scheduled team meetings and the use of crossfunctional teams that formed and dissolved as needed, had become the mechanisms for attending to ongoing operational issues.

At these meetings, the teams were able to see the connections between operational issues and the improvement projects, and they had all the teams' resources to redeploy if required. Gone were the separate operations review meetings at which departments pointed fingers across boundaries. In their place was a pragmatic alternative: The mechanisms for running the organization day to day had become the same as the mechanisms for managing change.

That is exactly as it should be.

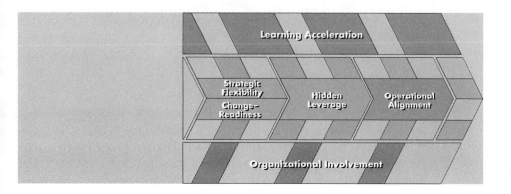

MEASURED MOVEMENTS

YOU GET WHAT YOU MEASURE

"We have found that one way to grab attention is to change the measurement system. Let us explore why. Data and theories drive organizational beliefs. Incorrect data are rarely caused by stupidity, but rather by beliefs and systems that reflect the pressures and needs of a previous era. These systems may have served organizations well under the old market rules of competition, but they become a menace when the rules of the game change. By providing misleading or incorrect numbers, the systems may perpetuate outworn beliefs and encourage organizations to make wrong decisions, or reinforce resistance to the 'right' decisions."

—*Charles Baden-Fuller and John Stopford, "Rejuvenating the Mature Business" (London: Routledge, 1992).*

Change requires an organization to acquire a new language, and "measures" is perhaps the most important word in the vocabulary. That's because measures often correspond to the strongest Triggers that drive some of the most critical unwritten rules.

As we've noted, people respond faster to changes in Triggers than to changes in Enablers, and very much faster than to attempts at changing noncore Motivators. So looking at measures is an important component of managing the operational aspects of change.

Consider the painful lesson learned by one Asian automobile assembler, which had competed successfully for years with its reliable, low-cost manufacturing ability despite a limited range of products. But changes in the market required it increasingly to compete on the basis of a greater variety of products, often customized. Investments were made in critical pieces of equipment, and employees were given additional training to plan and produce the greater variety of products. The new strategy was widely publicized throughout the firm and was well understood by all the employees. Once a week the general manager received a report on how well the special orders were being filled; once a month he convened a meeting of all managers to resolve problems.

Yet the new strategy was not taking hold as quickly as required. Small lots and special orders, which slowed overall production, were usually deferred or bunched together, and priority was given to longer runs of standard products.

Why?

The obstacle was found to be the general manager, who continued to get a summary report of the previous day's total production each morning. In the past, this had been the most important measure of total productivity and of operating costs. And the general manager continued to treat this daily report as he had for years, picking up the phone to purr at line managers when production was high, or to growl when it was low. His phone calls each morning could set the tone for every single manager's day.

So managers who looked good each morning by concentrating on total production numbers—even at the cost of not complying with the variety targets—could get away at the monthly meeting with some well-constructed explanation of resource bottlenecks. An important unwritten rule was: "It's more important to please the boss than to comply with the official strategy of the firm, so keep production totals high."

The breakthrough for change came when the general manager was persuaded to change his daily production report so that it showed the special orders that had been due the previous day and whether they were filled, while overall production totals were revealed only weekly. Now, when the general manager picked up the phone each morning, the purrs and growls reflected the special orders. And the new strategy was rapidly embraced.

Note that not only were new measures needed to reinforce priorities; some old measures had to be dropped to remove the unwritten rules associated with them—and to help employees concentrate on the new ones.

▓ THE RELUCTANT MANAGERS

Of course, managers are sometimes reluctant to let go of old measures. It may partly be their own change-resistance, but often it's because the old measures continue to be broadly relevant and they're loath to say goodbye to an old friend.

Even more commonly, the old measure is the Trigger in an M-E-T relationship that remains important to the manager. If managers continue to gain budgets based on the number of people shown as directly reporting to them on an organization chart, that measure will remain of intense importance even if it's not used for any other purpose—and even if the hierarchy suggested by the organization chart is highly spurious.

Indeed, the measure is likely to lead to all sorts of shenanigans when it comes to reaching agreements on formal changes in organization structure. The managers may not mind certain changes, but they'll fight to the death to maximize the number of people reporting directly to them on the new organizational chart—unless something sensible is done about it.

With such forces pushing behind them, measurement systems carry their own momentum. Once a measure is rolling along in the body of an organization, it tends to keep rolling, even when its formal use is less frequent. The momentum can only be reduced by moving the energy elsewhere, into a new measure.

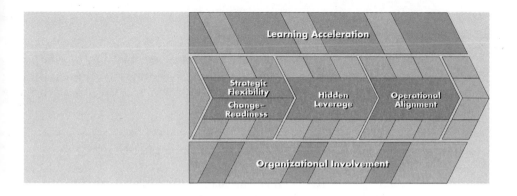

A SHARPER FOCUS

In deciding whether to invest in the stock of certain companies, you can look at the companies' financial performance, or you can look at the companies themselves. Most people look at the financial performance: they follow charts of stock price and other financial measures over time, and a statistical analysis of past performance is the basis for their investment decisions.

A few people, however, make their investment decisions by studying the operations of companies, looking at their products and evaluating their managers—on the theory that these attributes will ultimately be reflected in the share price.

If you don't have a good mental model of cause-and-effect in business, looking at the financials is all you can ever do. But if you really understand what can cause what, picking out the companies that are destined to succeed can make you rich: You invest before the rest of the pack and, at least in theory, make a great deal more money than they do.

Business managers seem to apply these same two broad approaches to managing their own organizations. When they don't have a real handle on how a business works, they fall back on trend-and-ratio analysis. Some managers have fallen back on financials and trend analyses because they haven't developed an additional—or alternative—measurement system based on the fundamentals of how the organization actually operates.

What a shame.

If increases in operating profit are the result of better products, more satisfied customers and more efficient operations, indicators other than profits are more valuable, because they would be leading indicators of the profits to come. Profits, of course, only show what has already happened.

 FINANCIAL MEASURES AREN'T ENOUGH

Arthur C. Martinez, chairman and CEO of Sears Merchandise Group, led the company out of the doldrums in which it was becalmed in the 1980s, in part by emphasizing alternative measurements. He emphasized the importance of setting ambitious goals and noted: "Such goals cannot be exclusively financial. As an indicator of an organization's ability to satisfy its customers and motivate its employees, financial performance usually lags behind other measurements."

Management should be devoting almost all its attention to such leading indicators and break its fixation with the financial consequences of performance, such as profit and loss, cash flow and the financial balance sheet. If improvements in products, customer service and effectiveness of operations is encouraged, for example, by better motivated and trained employees and by the organization's ability to create, acquire and apply knowledge, then managers should look for measures of these leading indicators.

■ WATCHING FOR IMPROVEMENT

The four universal measures of operational capability are throughput, operating costs, speed and quality in relation to customer expectations. Throughput is an indication of efficiency of use of the investment and available capacity; operating costs reflect the effectiveness of use of all operating inputs. Speed and quality measure response to customer needs. These measures apply to all types of operations, whether service operations or manufacturing operations. They're also closely linked to the satisfaction of at least two key stakeholders of the business: customers and owners.

It is primarily these measures that Business Process Reengineering seeks to improve. Indeed, the same could be said of the whole Industrial Engineering movement, from which much of Business Process Reengineering flowed. These four measures are good and valid, but like so many other management practices, they are part of a Newtonian model of business. In a world of flux, we need more Relativistic measures.

 ## THE IMPORTANCE OF MEASURES

"When you can measure what you are speaking about, and express it in numbers, you know something about it, but when you cannot measure it, when you cannot express it in numbers, your knowledge is of a meager and unsatisfactory kind."

—*"Popular Lectures and Addresses from 1891–1894," Baron Kelvin, mathematician and scientist.*

To begin with, managers working within a Relativistic model of business must measure the rate at which the operation capability is changing and improving: If the objective of the change process is to create an improved rate of improvement, you must measure what it is. There are many ways in which organizations measure the performance of the change process itself. But the key to their success is to ensure balance between leading indicators and lagging indicators and between measures of interest to those working within a process and those observing things from outside the process.

The External View of the change process will primarily be held by Sponsors—those who set or approve the general direction for change and have outcomes in mind from the start. For them, these outcomes are most likely to be defined in terms of the satisfaction of the principal stakeholders of the organization, or maybe the satisfaction of their personal Enablers: the CEO may focus on the board's satisfaction; the senior VPs on the CEO's.

For those involved in the change process, key Enablers—who allow the use of major resources—would also be external clients of the change process. The External View that these clients want of the process must be determined at the outset and revisited from time to time as the change proceeds.

The Internal View is needed by the Doers. Some Enablers of these Doers may also want more than just an External View of what's going on to reassure themselves of progress. The outcomes reflected in the Internal View would include satisfaction of the stakeholders in the performance of the process.

A balanced scorecard for the change process must reflect all four quadrants

	Change in-process measures (leading indicators)	Change process outcomes (lagging indicators)
External view (observers)	For example: Completion of analysis Acceptable plan Agreement with suppliers Creation of measurement system	For example: Satisfaction of stakeholders of the organization Improvements in products and operational capabilities
Internal view (participants)	For example: Commitment of allocation of necessary resources Number of people attending training courses	For example: New skills learned by change team Change team freed for next assignment

It's quite likely that, in a large integrated change process, some teams may have magnets that focus them more on one category of outcome than on another. Overall, however, the organization should be progressing on all fronts—and that should be reflected in a balanced score card of measurements.

■ THE SOFT STUFF

One reason why managers don't measure and manage supposedly "soft stuff," such as involvement of people and the learning ability of the organization, is the apparent lack of hard measures for such things. But that's a specious argument.

To exclude a variable from your equations is to imply that it has no impact or that it has an impact so negligible that it can be ignored in comparison to other, "harder," variables. To propose these days that the soft aspects of an organization have negligible impact is absurd, and widely recognized as such.

So it's far better to ascribe an approximate value based on a qualitative assessment than to ignore the variable altogether. In a metal foundry, experts take quick readings of temperature of very hot, molten metals by looking at the color. In the best restaurants, cooks assess when a sauce is ready by looking at its consistency. An expert industrial troubleshooter can pick up an accurate reading of a workplace just by walking around it.

We can do much better than that for many "soft" variables that affect the ability of an organization to accelerate its learning and improvement.

SIGNPOSTS TO MANAGING FOR OPERATIONAL ALIGNMENT

Trying to keep everything in alignment? Here are some guides:

1. Few managers have the luxury of building an operation from scratch. To provide continuity as you initiate change, ensure that the mechanisms for running the company are the same as those for managing change.

2. To change continuously, an organization must have both semipermanent structures, such as business processes, and change mechanisms, such as task forces that work across the structures.

3. To maintain operational alignment, the change mechanisms must embrace the design of business processes, the skills and motivation of the staff and the quality of the resources deployed.

4. Improving each element but ignoring the connections among them is never as effective as improving the whole system.

5. Follow three steps to improve the change processes:

- Tackle day-to-day burning issues, such as customer problems and equipment failures.

- Set up teams to address all processes that cry out for improvement.

- Set up teams to seek improvements in the underlying infrastructure, such as information systems, training and performance appraisal.

6. Then, take three steps to align the change processes:

- Set up an improvement team to align overall specifications and set guidelines for every team.

- Set up a multifunctional team for each major task, initially at the process level, then at the infrastructure level.

- Institute a formal integration process.

7. Use a balanced scorecard to measure the change process. Develop measures that go beyond financial performance, which is a lagging indicator.

CHAPTER 5

Learning Acceleration

Strategic Flexibility

Change–Readiness

Hidden Leverage

Operational Alignment

Organizational Involvement

MANAGING FOR ORGANIZATIONAL INVOLVEMENT

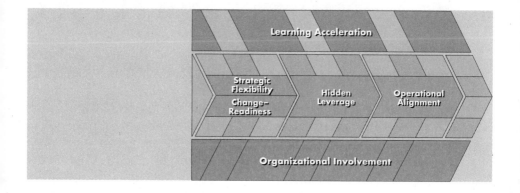

THE ARCHITECTURE OF INVOLVEMENT

Every morning, hundreds of thousands of office workers funnel from the suburbs into the business districts of Manhattan, London, Tokyo, Hong Kong, Bombay and other cities.

In Bombay alone, as the rush hour ends, something remarkable occurs. At workers' homes, after breakfast tables have been cleared and children sent to school, spouses, parents or friends of the office workers prepare hot meals. And just before lunchtime, those hundreds of thousands of workers toiling away in the skyscrapers have that freshly cooked meal delivered to their office—still warm. Before they return home, lunch containers will already be washed and back on the kitchen shelves at home. Yet there are no delivery vans; the trips are made by couriers using public transportation, which is what makes the service affordable to the office workers. And the courier who calls at the house is not the one who delivers to the office, nor do the couriers have any communications devices to talk to each other. And no central controller directs.

It's amazing—and remarkably like another phenomenon, the Internet. It relies on public lines, low cost, no central controller—and yet is able to make connections between people all over the place. Most people imagine that anything as complicated as a global computer network has to be designed and run by some central authority, but *The Economist* was absolutely accurate when it called the Internet the "accidental superhighway."

At the Santa Fe Institute in New Mexico, scientists exploring the characteristics of systems of many different kinds—biological species, chemical systems, computer networks—have concluded that not only do such complex systems not require a central controller, but they evolve precisely because they do not have a central controller. An economic parallel is the extent to which free market systems seem more efficient and productive than a centrally planned economy.

But Lee Kwan Yew, the architect of Singapore's remarkable development, and experts on the Japanese, South Korean and Taiwanese economic and political systems, have recently drawn attention to the important role of strong central guidance in the admirable growth of these Asian economies. And some important management thinkers, including Elliot Jacques, who was among the earliest and strongest proponents of bottom-up management, now caution that a command hierarchy does serve a valuable purpose. In our zeal for more empowered, flatter organizations, these experts warn, we should not throw the good out with the bad.

Once again, you need a balanced approach, a Middle Way. In some situations business organizations may indeed be able to function without any evidence of a center. But they're hard to imagine. And in rare cases, organizations with pure command-and-control structures may be able to tap the energy of all their members and adapt, change and grow sufficiently.

But most organizations wanting to become Accelerating Organizations need a structure that falls somewhere between pure decentralized autonomy and pure command and control—in other words, an architecture that encourages widespread involvement while maintaining centers of accountability.

We call this architecture "Optimally Aligned Networked Teams."

■ REDESIGNING THE PYRAMIDS

Historically, companies that were vertically integrated hierarchies sought efficiency by owning and controlling most of the resources and services they needed. Henry Ford's River Rouge plant in Detroit had iron ore brought in by barges at one end and finished cars ran off the assembly line at the other end.

Such firms were highly efficient. Ford, for example, was able to sell cars profitably at less than half the price of his competitors and so changed the face of the automobile market. But this structure engendered rigidity, as Ford's famous "Any color so long as it's black" makes clear.

Contrast General Motors, which still has a hard time changing in response to customer needs, with Chrysler, which has proved admirably nimble in the last decade. Where GM produces 70 percent of the components for its cars, Chrysler buys 70 percent outside. Similarly, apparel and footwear manufacturers—Benetton, Nike, Reebok and others—can offer a vast and changing variety of designs because they don't own their manufacturing facilities. They sit at the hub of vast worldwide networks that connect efficient manufacturers with the needs and wants of customers.

Networked organizations are not only able to offer greater variety—note that Levi Strauss is now offering customized jeans—but they seem to make more money doing so. Look at the computer industry. *Fortune* magazine (Feb. 8, 1993) published a comparison of the return on equity of 17 firms in the computer industry and their degree of vertical integration.

The analysis showed a remarkably consistent correlation. The pyramidal, vertically integrated companies—Unisys, DEC and IBM—sat at the bottom. Companies that rely much more on others—Dell and Sun, for example—were near the top. (Dell, by the way, owns no plants at all and leases two small factories to assemble computers from outsourced parts.) The highest returns on equity were from small networked firms, such as Cisco and Quantum, suppliers to the computer companies that are at the nodes of little networks of their own suppliers: intentionally working with other specialists rather than doing too much themselves.

Yet many corporations have found it difficult to design practical organization structures that break away from the classic bureaucratic hierarchy and reflect all the dimensions that need to be managed in any reasonably large and complex organization. Should the firm be divided along product lines, market lines or geographical lines? Who should have control over people and resources: the regional manager, product manager, or market manager?

Trying to resolve such quandaries in the 1970s led to a spate of matrix organizations, in which a given individual reported to two bosses, perhaps a geographic boss and a product boss. These structures proved horribly difficult to manage, and often horribly difficult to work in. All those "solid lines" and "dotted lines" tended to degrade into tugs and counter pulls, divided loyalties and all sorts of confusion. Robert Palmer, the head of Digital Equipment, blames his firm's matrix structure for severely delaying its shift from minicomputers to personal computers.

Many other top managers agree that matrix organizations are time consuming and bureaucratic, that they institutionalize dithering and leave everybody disappointed, because nobody can satisfactorily serve two masters.

One of the worst problems with the matrix architecture is that it applies the Master-Servant model to every important dimension of the business. That's unfortunate, because even when the Master-Servant model is applied in a single clear chain of command and control, it often stifles initiative and creativity—especially when managers in the organization act as if authority and control are indispensable for getting anything done. When people within an organization are caught in two authoritarian chains of command, the compound effect can be stultifying.

So networked organizations may be attractive in principle, but the classic way of achieving them doesn't work very well. Let's look at alternatives.

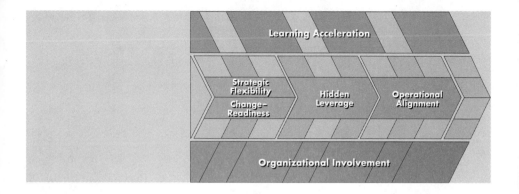

COMBS, GRIDS, FANS AND WEBS

All organizations larger than 10 or 15 people seem to beg to be broken into pieces, so that each can concentrate on what it's best equipped to do, needs to do and—in the best organizations—wants to do. So optimal compartmentalizing is the first focus of the classical designer of Newtonian organization structures.

First the corporation is split into Strategic Business Units, then into task specializations at the operating level. The next step is to decide how all these different components should be linked together. This is the step that has changed the most in the last few years.

For most of this century the automatic linking of tasks was into business functions, such as R&D, Production and Sales. Recently, however, business engineers have been excited about clustering together all the tasks relating to a given major business process, such as product creation or customer service. This appears an attractive route because it allows the organization to cut across all the "silos" or "chimneys" of the classic functional organization. Some have gone so far as to suggest that functions should be thrown away and organizations should be structured only around processes.

But such a shift does not fundamentally change the structure of the organization: It still remains like a set of lines, each separated from the other, all held together at the top. We call this model the Comb architecture.

The Comb architecture

■ THE COMB ARCHITECTURE

The Comb is based on the seemingly attractive notion that the teeth of the comb—whether business units, functions or business processes—can be self-sufficient and held solely accountable for their performance by the person at the top, where all the rods are held together.

This was the model by which Harold Geneen ran ITT successfully for ages. He set objectives for all the units of ITT, received reports on their performance and rewarded or penalized the managers. It worked for a long while because the units of ITT, a highly diversified conglomerate, were independent of each other and the major perceived link between them was their contribution to the corporate financial pot.

 SIMPLISTIC COMBING

Lou Gerstner resisted applying the Comb to IBM, even though it seemed to some people the most workable approach. "Someone drew a line and said, 'We're going to have good performance and decentralization.' It's a simplification I don't accept."
—Business Week, *Oct. 4, 1993*

■ THE GRID

Few reengineering aficionados have gone so far as to propose a pure Comb structure around processes; most of them recognize that functions are good at what functions are good at. Instead they've proposed some combined structure in which the functions are retained but the process structure is overlaid on top of them. It's another form of the matrix—basically two Comb structures laid one atop the each other, forming what we call a Grid.

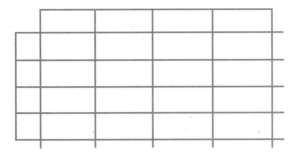

The Grid architecture

The trouble with these modern Grids is that although functions laid across processes may appear very different from functions laid across markets or countries (the classic matrix), the management problems remain similar.

The methods of encouraging people's involvement have not really changed; the mental model of Master-Servant has not really gone away, either. Indeed, the terms in which many reengineers describe the way these lateral connections will be managed—by Process Owners, for example—make us worry that such organizations will continue to apply the traditional notions of managing people and so create only another version of a matrix organization: difficult to manage and inflexible in the long run.

Yes, networks are attractive. But to make them work, many managers will require a new mental model for how cooperation and deep commitment can be obtained from vendors, employees and others. The model that has to be "unlearned" is the one that suggests that it is necessary to have control over those whose cooperation is needed, either through ownership or through line authority. In the new model, managers have to obtain full cooperation without resorting to either form of control.

▇ THE FAN

An emerging structure that does break from the old Master-Servant mindset is the Fan. It retains the important benefits of the Comb architecture but enhances the classic hierarchy with different, more fluid forms of organizing work and people. The Fan is our preferred architecture for any accelerating organization.

The Fan has fairly rigid spokes, linked by flexible, lateral threads. In other words, the Fan architecture comprises semiper-

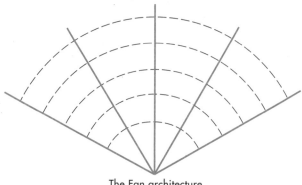

The Fan architecture

manent organizational structures overlaid with temporary structures—our preferred approach in our earlier discussion of operationalizing change.

The organization adopted by Honda is actually a Fan: Honda is basically divided into three companies with separate balance sheets: one for R&D, another for Engineering, a third for producing and selling products. But anything of significance is assigned to a team to accomplish—and such teams always have representatives from all three spokes of the Fan.

Some tasks are much larger and longer than others, such as developing a major product or setting up an operation in another country. So the members of such a team are dedicated to the team and stay with it a long time, sometimes even years. Other tasks are smaller or shorter and may have teams whose members are also working on another team or task at the same time.

In the Fan architecture, the spokes converge at the bottom, where there is a center of coordination and a team in charge. At Honda, the CEO and his executive team share a large office at the company's headquarters in Tokyo. They consider one of their most important roles to be the formation and support of the lateral teams that get things done. At Asea Brown Boveri, a decentralized worldwide network of companies, the CEO, Percy Barnevik, operates with a small staff from Zurich, fostering connections, where necessary, among the far-flung companies of the group.

Organizations know how to manage the largely traditional spokes of the Fan architecture; it's the soft, lateral strands that are new and more difficult to manage. Teams, task forces, worldwide centers of excellence—such as Ford has recently established—and practice areas (used by many consulting firms) are mechanisms for providing the lateral connections. All these require people to work together and relate to each other in a collaborative mode for achieving a common goal, and to do so in spite of the internal competition that the spokes of the Fan may engender: competition for budgetary resources, for bonuses and for fulfilling regional or functional objectives.

■ THE WEB

The Web has intersecting and flexible threads in many directions.

The flexible threads are teams of people working together to accomplish something toward the overall objectives of their organization. The net has a central node, as in a spider web, that identifies the existence of the organization. And in an increasingly networked world, many nets will intersect, so the boundaries of organizations will become increasingly unclear.

The only way you would know that one organization was distinct from another would be by recognizing the nodes: points around which you could see a convergence of activity. At the fringes, the various nets would run into each other; it wouldn't be easy to say who or what belonged where or to whom.

Although such Webs are still largely theoretical, they're not science fiction. Peter Drucker pointed out in *The Wall Street Journal* (Mar. 29, 1995) that fewer and fewer people are working as employees of organizations. Instead they serve various organizations on an as-needed basis, often working with more than one organization at a given time. To which parts of the web do they belong? And smaller firms that serve several larger firms

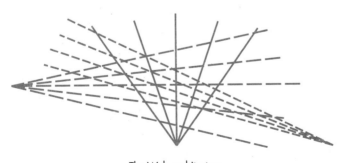

The Web architecture

are integral members of each's network, as we saw in the computer industry.

 AN EXISTING WEB

There is at least one large, successful organization that in many ways is a Web, and it has been growing for a quarter of a century at 20 to 50 percent a year. It now holds 23,000 institutions in 200 countries and territories, and its market-leading products are used by 465 million people, who make more than seven billion transactions a year worth $800 billion. That amounts to the single largest block of consumer purchasing power in the world.

If it were on the stock market, this Web would be worth about $150 billion. But it can't be bought, sold or raided. There is very little centralized control, and the portion of business created by all the components of the organization is theirs and theirs alone.

Its name? Visa.

Widespread adoption of Webs may still be a long time off, although the Internet is already spawning some intriguing Web organizations. What's important about Webs is not so much the detail as the trend.

However appropriate the Fan is right now as the infrastructure for an Accelerating Organization, it's unlikely to last more than a few decades. But, for the moment, it's the best networking architecture we've got.

Yet for the Fan to work properly, we need teamwork. So let's look at Networks of Teams.

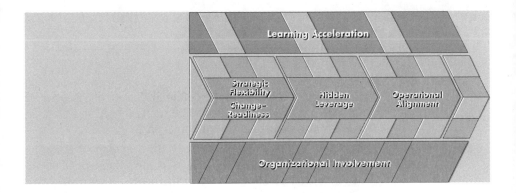

LAYING
FOUNDATIONS
OF TEAMWORK

Within large organizations, networked teams have become pretty much a necessity, for at least two reasons.

First, many organizational tasks these days have to be performed by large networks of people, often because new information technology enables the task to be done much more rapidly and flexibly by a network of people than by a traditional series of autonomous departments. This is true both of service industries such as banking, insurance and travel services and of the development and service functions in manufacturing industries.

Second, consistent evidence makes clear that team-based organizations produce better results than traditional, hierarchical organizations, even where the latter approach still works.

It is possible, for example, to run an efficient manufacturing organization by breaking up the process into specialized tasks, setting standards for the tasks, assigning them to people, then supervising those people and rewarding or penalizing them depending on their individual performance. Many organizations continue to manage in this traditional way. But time and again it has been demonstrated, by comparing plants in the same industry or within the same company, that the performance of tradi-

THE POWER OF ONE

The Houston Rockets, winners of the National Basketball Association championship in 1994 and 1995, will be remembered as a team whose whole greatly exceeded the sum of its parts.

Five or six teams in the league had more pure individual talent than the Rockets, even though the Rockets' center, Hakeem Olajuwomn, was one of the greatest players in the game. What brought the Rockets victory was that they understood that to win they needed to be a knucklehead-free, selfless team.

They called it the Power of One: the importance of playing together, of submerging ego, statistics and other personal gain for the opportunity to win it all.

Chucky Brown, one of the team's best role players, commented: "When you think of the 90's athlete, things are supposed to be always crazy, right? But I think it's completely unprofessional to think that points are the only thing. It's unprofessional to think, 'I gotta get mine.' There's no place here for that on this team."

—*Bryan Burwell, sports commentator, USA Today, June 13, 1995.*

tional plants cannot compete with that of team-based organizations.

What do these team-based plants look like? They generally have a number of semi-autonomous teams of 10 to 20 people, each responsible for a part of the plant or a stage of the production process. The teams consist of people who collectively take responsibility for the output, timeliness, cost and quality of their piece of the action. They assign jobs among themselves, are often multiskilled and are able to back each other up and rotate assignments. They determine their own training needs and often take responsibility for hiring members and disciplining their own.

In many cases, they also determine how they will be internally led and select their own leaders or coordinators. All the teams nominate representatives to plantwide councils that shape plantwide policies. Generally small specialist groups provide the teams with support as required for training, technical services and information services. And the plant manager is at the node of this network of teams, ensuring that goals are clarified, that teams integrate where they need to and get the support they require. He is also responsible for external communications and upholding plantwide standards.

LESSONS OF TEAMWORK

Procter & Gamble, which established its first team-based plants in the 1960s, was always very tight-lipped about them. By the mid-1980s, when it had 18 such plants operating, it confirmed that they were 30 to 40 percent more productive than the company's traditional plants and significantly more adaptable to the changing needs of the business.

Corning's plant in Blacksburg, Virginia, which produces ceramic cores for catalytic converters, is run by work teams, in direct contrast to its sister plant in Erwin, New York, which is organized on traditional lines. The results are very encouraging: Blackburg turned a modest profit in the first eight months of production, instead of an anticipated startup loss. In each successive year, the plant delivered more than the annual plan required—in terms of material yield, on-time delivery, cost per unit, and defective parts per million—turning in a far better performance than Erwin.

At hundreds of other companies, from automobiles and textiles to building materials, glass and food, the same lessons have been learned.

FIVE TYPES OF SUCCESSFUL TEAMS

Within Fan organizations, five main types of teams have been used successfully:

Semi-autonomous teams of operators, also known as "high-performance teams" or "self-managed teams." Relatively permanent structures, such teams are responsible for a piece of the operation.

Project teams, such as product development teams or teams to establish an operation or a system, or consulting assignment teams. These are ad hoc and temporary; they disband once their task is done. They invariably have a full-time core group and many part-time members.

Problem-solving teams. These are created to diagnose a problem and design a solution, which may then require one or many project teams to implement it. The members of problem-solving teams often participate part time, but in a crisis they could work full time, functioning like a project team.

Management teams. They create and integrate other teams. Coordinated Design Groups and Integration Teams, described earlier in this book, are examples of management teams. The Honda Executive Board is another.

Learning teams, such as Quality Circles, Centers of Excellence or Consulting Practices. Members interact periodically and are likely to do so increasingly through interactive information systems. These groups need to direct themselves and to feel driven to produce some deliverables if they are to acquire the character of a team; otherwise they can all too easily degenerate into social clubs.

 ## PROJECT TEAMS AT HONDA

Project teams are used extensively at Honda to accomplish many different types of things. Honda likes the concept because it focuses teams on time-bound outcomes, brings people together from different parts of the company, provides them opportunities for learning and offers a great way to develop leaders who can manage in the Honda way—creatively, through teams and projects across the organization rather than bureaucratically, through individuals and tasks within departments.

The Executive Board members of Honda spend a good deal of time subjectively evaluating personnel and matching the things the firm needs to get done with the abilities and development needs of people. From these discussions spring the project teams.

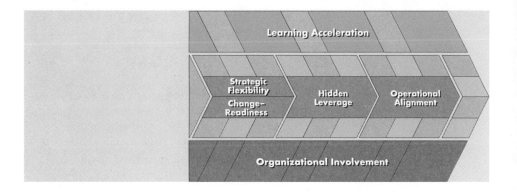

GETTING
EVERYTHING
INTO ALIGNMENT

If you know you want a Fan architecture and you know that teamwork is a necessary precondition for the network to function optimally, why is it more than a trivial exercise for every would-be Accelerating Organization to implement networked teams? What can be done to make such changes more smoothly?

Remember the five barriers that must be overcome when managing for change-readiness:

- People throughout the organization must feel that change is necessary.
- People must consider the proposed change appropriate.
- People have to feel they've been acknowledged as individuals.
- People have to have the skills to achieve the goals.
- The system must support the required behaviors.

To overcome the barriers to implementing networked teams, you need to satisfy each of these five criteria. And that's often a major problem unless it's tackled systematically: You need to draw on many skills covered earlier in the book—managing for strategic flexibility, change-readiness and hidden leverage.

JAPANESE TEAMWORK IN THE U.S.

How much does Honda's much-admired teamwork have to do with the Japanese culture? To explore this, we visited Honda's plant in Marysville, Ohio, after studying Honda in Japan. Honda's American success is well known; its Accord has traded places with the Ford Taurus for years as the best-selling car in the United States, while Honda's Acura division has led the J.D. Power Customer Satisfaction Index.

We met Toshikata Amino, Executive Vice President of Honda America, who has been in the United States since the inception of Honda's team-based operations in Marysville, which are managed almost entirely by Americans. The key to creating the successful US organization was to change the orientation of the US managers from managing individuals and tasks to managing teams and projects, he said.

He used the analogy of a team sport: Too many US managers are like a basketball coach who concentrates solely on the opponent's basket and rewards or punishes his players for their scoring performance. Any good coach knows that everyone need not score, that delivering the ball to the scorers and stopping the other team are equally important.

The obvious solution of measuring assists and steals and so on, he said, only leads to concern in the players' minds about the relative worth of the different numbers. So a lot of emotional energy and managerial time is spent on fair distribution of rewards rather than on winning as a team. This is unavoidable if your mental model of good management is to hold individuals accountable and use monetary reward as a prime means of motivation.

Better are systems that divide responsibility for performance equally among the members of the organization. And the more arithmetical the measurement of performance, the more objective the system appears to be. But these systems compel people to focus on their individual output, and they reinforce a culture of individualism at the cost of real teamwork, he continued. Many managers with one hand try and promote teamwork through communications and training while with the other they make it more difficult, through the performance measurement and reward systems.

Satisfying the first criterion—being persuasive that change from the Comb or Grid architecture is necessary—is largely a matter of creating awareness by good communication. The goal is to create a dissatisfaction with the current reality of hierarchical bureaucracy. This should be easy, for traditional structures are creaking at the seams trying to accommodate new styles of working. However, following the philosophy that The Journey Is the Destination, you need to start as you intend to continue—and cast any communications in a form consistent with the desired new architecture.

You don't want to fall into the trap of the CEO who autocratically told his people that they must act as if they were empowered. The Corporate Communications department should be drawn into this discussion early on, not so much to help shape the content, as it will expect, but to help with style—which needs to be based on a two-way communication process with face-to-face interaction. That will convey tacit as well as explicit content.

The second change-readiness criterion—that networked teams are appropriate—is often more difficult to satisfy. Most people within an organization genuinely don't know what it would feel like to be on a networked team. Worse, their experiences with so-called teams have often actually been experiences of loose confederations of individuals; as a result, for many people, the terms *teams* and *teamwork* carry the wrong connotations. The most powerful method of overcoming all this confusion seems to be to tie everything back to shared vision—using the approaches of Strategic Flexibility and Change-Readiness.

It's extraordinary how often people's personal visions of what they'd like their organization to become has at its core a sense of greater camaraderie and mutual support.

At a recent visioning exercise, the members of a team drawn from Arthur D. Little and Innovation Associates—companies well known for the friendships that develop among colleagues—were amazed at just how highly they each valued the personal relationships that they had developed with colleagues both within our companies and with our clients. And they wanted those relationships to be still stronger and more numerous. For many participants in this exercise, this was the first time that "personal" driver had been openly shared.

The same situation prevails in many other organizations—and the skill of the change manager is to tap this shared desire.

So the first step of creating an emotional magnet to pull the organization onward and upward toward networked teams is not to communicate the vision of networked teams, but to see if a shared vision of networked teams naturally emerges from the organization itself, using any of the Selling, Testing, Consulting or Co-creating modes discussed under Strategic Flexibility.

Often some variant of networked teams will emerge, for purely pragmatic reasons, and that will provide some Aspiration and Inspiration components for a series of magnets. Discussions about the Perspiration component—how the vision will be achieved—will lead groups to consider what kinds of changes would be needed to the existing infrastructure. Such discussions will help the organization pull itself over the second hurdle of change-readiness.

The third hurdle—acknowledging people's past roles—can be important when migrating to networked teams. Inevitably the change involves the breakdown of many fiefdoms, and an apparent loss of power for some. The seven steps of letting go (covered in Chapter 3) should be sufficient to help an organization move on.

The fourth hurdle—ensuring people have the skills to work in networked teams—will require training (and retraining, and more retraining).

Which brings us to the fifth and, for some, the highest hurdle—removing systemic barriers to networked teams. This can be a major headache.

The three most common disconnects that come to light seem to be inappropriate job designs, ill-conceived performance measures and unsuitable compensation systems. Let's spend a moment on the latter.

You may remember that the approaches to Hidden Leverage do not all that often lead to money: In our experience, on the list of Motivators for a typical organization, money tends to score fourth, fifth or sixth. Generally a bonus or salary increase is perceived as "nice to have," but rarely is it the factor that drives people day to day to act in particular ways (except for groups working almost entirely on commission).

On the other hand, bonuses and salary increases bring recognition. And recognition, in one form or another, tends to be high on the list of Motivators in any organization.

If financial incentives are an organization's only formal means of recognizing its employees, other than occasional and increasingly rare career advancement, then such incentives end up carrying a relevance totally disproportionate to their apparent importance. So be highly skeptical the next time one of your colleagues mouths the hackneyed phrase: "Money isn't really all that important around here." Money may not be, but what it represents may turn out to be paramount.

What's the solution? The details, naturally, will be specific to your own organization, but there is a broad class of solution: Come up with an appropriate set of performance measures and then develop reward systems that employees can tie into.

To do that, you need to avoid like the plague the classic solution of calling in a compensation specialist: The problem is not so much the compensation part as the specialism. They tend to focus on bonus systems, contingent compensation, remuneration packages and so forth to the exclusion of all else. When you're trying to get alignment between different aspects of your organization, allowing an outsider to come in and apparently optimize one aspect in splendid isolation of the rest can be worse than foolhardy—it can be dangerous. It can totally undermine all your attempts at systems thinking, and totally disrupt your organization's ability to adopt a new architecture.

If you can find some genuine reward specialists, however, well, grab them—they're rare.

 ## PROBLEMS WITH HAY POINTS

Some side effects of the original Hay Points system had to be seen to be believed. Compensation was linked to the number of Points your job was worth, and the more subordinates you had, the more Points the Hay system applied to your job. It doesn't take Einstein to see how this might affect attempts to create fluid networks of teams that formed and reformed where needed without benefit of a fixed boss.

So consider things on a broader front than just money. Evaluate the top five Motivators in your organization and aim to create Triggers tied primarily to the top three—perhaps job security, respect and exciting work. If your organization turns out not to be so homogeneous as to have consistent Motivators across it, then take account of that by constructing systems that reward differently those with different Motivators—in the same way that dual career tracks are designed to do. And if you find that your organization is using remuneration as its primary form of formal recognition, wean it off by instituting a range of alternatives, such as public award ceremonies.

REWARDS REFERENCE

Stuck for alternative rewards? A great quick read is "1001 Ways to Reward Employees," by Bob Nelson *(New York: Workman, 1995)*.

Even when a primary Motivator appears difficult to satisfy—job security, for example—explore just how far it can be pushed. Most organizations that proclaim "the promise of job security is no longer a gift in our power to give" have missed the point. Offering even limited job security is better than offering none at all. For the best performers to be rewarded with a guaranteed job for at least two years, for example, means that for the next 12 months, those people are likely to keep their heads down and concentrate on their work. If, at the end of that time, they are once again recognized as being worthy of the guarantee of work for two years, they will once again keep their heads down, and so on. Provided that only the better performers get such a guarantee (while the majority of the employees get, say, one year), then almost any organization can use limited job security as a reward mechanism.

SOUTHWEST AIRLINES

Ever flown Southwest Airlines? It has the best customer service record in the industry. And it turns around planes faster than anyone else in the business. While you're waiting for your flight, you can observe the effect of the almost palpable teamwork among the agents, flight deck, maintenance personnel, ground staff, baggage handlers and cabin crew—who all hustle to make this happen. On occasion, we've seen the cabin crew helping to load luggage. On what other airline would that happen?

Southwest Airlines is one large team within which are many smaller teams. Some stay together for long periods—the sales office, for instance. Some come together for short periods and disband as soon their job is done—as when turning around a plane. Southwest also has the distinction of being the highest-performing stock in any industry in the United States: its share prices appreciated 21,775 percent between 1972 and 1992, even though the airline industry has been going through hard times.

Discussing Southwest's success, the CEO, Herb Kelleher, once said: "People will write me and complain, 'Hey, I got terminated or put on probation for purely subjective reasons.' And I'll say: 'Right! Those are the important reasons! We believe in taking subjective decisions!' Another way I put it is this: Very often the most valuable things in life aren't quantifiable."

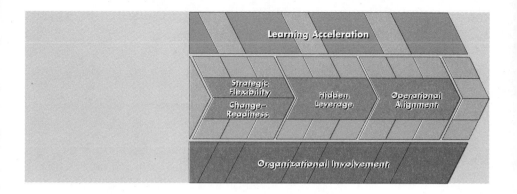

BINDING THE ORGANIZATION TOGETHER

With all these changes under way, how can you gain assurance that the new architecture will hold together? How can you feel secure that the whole structure won't just break apart or degrade into anarchic chaos, what with all these fluid teams, evolving networks, empowerment and lack of command and control.

The answer, in a word, is Trust.

Hearing that, many busy, practical managers may feel like turning to the next chapter. Trust seems so nebulous; like faith, you either have it or you don't. Not so, we say.

There's a whole lot of practical stuff you can do to build trust. So pragmatic managers, read on.

 ## INFORMALITY LEADS TO TRUST

In a survey of multinationals published in June 1995, *The Economist* pointed that firms are beginning to resemble networks of alliances—even on the inside. And with the widespread shift to informal controls, trust is becoming much more of an issue. Charles Handy, in "Trust and the Virtual Organization" (*Harvard Business Review*, May–June 1995), asks: "How do you manage people whom you do not see?" And, we might add, whom you don't own and cannot fire, because they may not be your employees? Handy's simple answer: "By trusting them."

Why are people starting to pay so much attention to Trust? Ten years ago, people were still looking for the common denominators of excellent companies, and Robert Levering, Milton Moskowitz, and Michael Katz produced a best seller, "The 100 Best Companies to Work for in America" (Addison-Wesley, 1984). Then various analysts decided to have a look at just how well those companies performed relative to the general business community.

One looked at earnings per share, comparing the Levering "100 Best" with the S&P 500 Index. Another considered total return on investment and contrasted the "100 Best" with the Russell 3000 Index. In each case, the companies that were "great places to work" also turned out to be great places to invest: Over the previous decade, the "100 Best" companies had consistently outperformed the rest.

"100 best" vs. S&P 500 (1985)

"100 best" vs. the rest (1993)

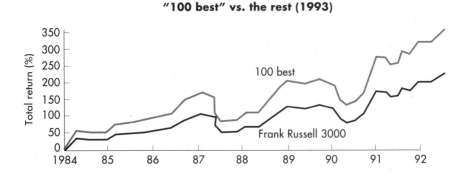

So what are the implications of that statistical correlation for managers. Does being a great place to work lead to higher performance? Or if a company performs well, does that eventually lead to it becoming a great company to work for? Which is the cause, and which the effect?

Interestingly, there does appear to be a broad answer to that question.

Ten years after the original survey, Levering returned to the "100 Best" companies and surveyed them again, along with some other companies. Although there were some changes to the "100 Best," he found no examples of companies that started off as not being great places to work, became high performers and then became great places to work. On the other hand, he did find companies that started off as being great places to work, were not performing well, and turned into high-performing companies that remained great places to work.

Still not fully convinced? Consider a U.S. Department of Labor study in 1993. It compared 75 "progressive" organizations from the Forbes 500 (defining them as firms with significant worker involvement, training, job flexibility, teams, profit sharing and so on) with 75 "less progressive" organizations from the Forbes 500 (defining these as traditional, hierarchical, managed by command and control). The companies examined represented many different industries.

Over five years, the less progressive firms had an average annual increase in profits of 2.6 percent, the progressive firms 10.8 percent. The less progressive firms averaged 10.7 percent in sales growth; the progressive firms 17.5 percent. Similarly, a look at 30 unionized steelmakers found the less progressive organizations had uptime of 88 percent, the progressive firms 98 percent. And the Department of Labor reported that, in a study of productivity at 1,000 machining firms, output was 9 percent higher when workers were responsible for writing their own operating procedures.

Need more evidence? Consider the General Motors plant in Fremont, California that managed to double its productivity after introducing a management system designed to involve people. Absenteeism dropped from about 25 percent to about 4 percent, grievances a similar amount, the perceived quality of working life soared, and productivity climbed almost to the level of the Toyota Motor Corporation's plant in Japan.

And look what happened at Merck's Canadian unit: Management asked the employees to improve the way work was done so as to enable them to lead more balanced and satisfying lives—more time at home, more satisfying work at the office, and so on. This was an unusual approach, because the focus of work process improvement, as in reengineering, is invariably on customer satisfaction and the bottom line.

Task forces of managers and employees came up with a host of improvements: streamlining workflows, eliminating redundant reports and more. The outcome resembled the results of a top-down reengineering, and the employees improved their own lives.

First Tennessee National, a banking company in Memphis, had the same experience as Merck.

 ## LEFT HAND, MEET RIGHT HAND

A curious finding was reported by *The New York Times* (Feb. 19, 1995) in a survey of senior executives. Nine of 10 executives told researchers that people are a company's most important resource; 98 percent said improved employee performance would enhance the bottom line.

But when asked to rank the strategies most likely to bring success, these same executives put the people issues—performance and investment in the work force—near the bottom. It's probably not that these executives are hypocrites; they just don't know any really practical things that they could to do to improve the soft sides of their companies.

That brings us back to Trust. From all his work on the "100 Best" companies, Levering developed a model of what translates into a great organization to work for. He also found Trust to be the key element. And he went much further, determining the factors that contribute to the likelihood of trustful relationships—and describing a way of assessing an organization with respect to these factors.

We'll look at those in the next chapter.

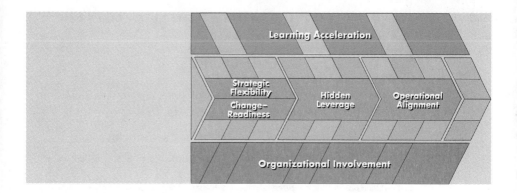

HOW STRONG ARE THE BONDS?

Let's be clear from the start that the Levering Trust model is not about employee satisfaction, although improved employee satisfaction is likely to be an outcome of improving trust.

Nor is improving trust about special human resources practices, such as providing child-care centers or free cafeterias. Rather, the Trust model focuses on the condition that Levering has demonstrated is at the heart of a good workplace—the quality of relationships within it.

At the heart of the Levering model is Organizational Involvement, which is the outcome of three interconnected relationships: between employees and management, between employees and their jobs and among employees themselves. Each of these three has a key element.

Relationship	Key Element
Employees and Management	Trust
Employees and their jobs	Pride
Employees and other employees	Camaraderie

THE COMPONENTS OF TRUST

Credibility: The extent to which employees can believe, rely on and have faith in management.

Fairness: How level the playing field appears to employees.

Respect: The underlying attitudes that employees see expressed in management's actions toward them.

The relationship between management and the employee is the most important for an organization. For it to succeed, Trust is essential—and comes down to three major factors.

First, management must have credibility in the eyes of employees. Executives should be perceived to be competent, to have a clear view of where the organization is going and to understand how to get there. Nothing is more demoralizing than working for people who don't have a firm grasp of the business. Management must also be able to handle delicate issues, such as conflicts between the unwritten and the explicit rules of the organization. And employees want to work for executives who tell the truth, even during difficult times.

Roger Hale, the CEO of Tennant Company, the world's leading maker of industrial floor maintenance equipment, says that when his firm faced tough times, he increased the number of meetings with employees. Because rumors tend to spread more during hard times, he says, management should be even more accessible then.

To earn people's confidence, executives must also be willing to listen to hard truths, avoiding a "shoot the messenger" atmosphere. A number of companies have institutionalized forums where executives submit to difficult employee questioning. Pitney Bowes, for instance, has annual "jobholders meetings," similar to annual shareholders meetings. At these gatherings, top executives meet with groups of employees throughout the company; the employees who ask the best written and the best oral questions are given $50 savings bonds—and an employee group determines the winners.

Such a meeting helps establish an environment in which managers can demonstrate that they are willing to listen to employee concerns rather than hide behind layers of bureaucracy. But willingness to listen is not enough to establish credibility.

Executives must also earn a reputation for delivering on their promises and show overall consistency in their behavior: They must Walk Their Talk.

At Pitney Bowes, management makes sure that each question asked in the jobholders meeting is followed up, that the employee who asked the question is given a report of the status of his or her concern and that written reports are made to larger groups of employees when appropriate.

The second element of Trust is fairness.

Employees must perceive that the playing field is level, that promotions and pay are based on merit and contributions rather than on political maneuvering and that cuts, when necessary, will be made fairly and objectively.

If someone feels unfairly treated, they must believe they have ways to recourse. IBM has long had ombudsmen within the office of the chief executive who investigate accusations of unfairness brought by lower-level employees. This has helped create an atmosphere in which supervisors understand that they are not allowed to take advantage of their employees.

Third, Trust involves respect. Employees must feel that they are respected and supported as individuals. Partly this stems from employees being given a lot of responsibility for their jobs and involvement in decisions that affect their work. Training must provide opportunities for employees to develop skills. Management also shows respect by encouraging and responding to employees' suggestions and ideas.

Many companies made great strides in this area because of the total quality movement. In many firms, small groups of employees meet regularly to brainstorm and figure out how to put their ideas into practice.

■ PRIDE IS ALMOST AS CRITICAL AS TRUST

While fostering Trust in the management-employee relationship is the most important element in creating a great workplace, attention must also be given to the employee's relationship with the job itself. The key here is *pride*.

People develop pride when they feel their work has special meaning—that what they are doing is not "just a job." And to feel this way, employees need to believe that they personally make a difference. They need a sense that their product or service has some significance to others. Managers can cultivate this attitude by helping employees see how their tasks fit into the big picture or how customers use their products.

At Moog, an aerospace manufacturer, top management designed a factory to make certain that production employees could literally see how their work fit into the overall product: The parking area encircles the building. So employees have to walk through various parts of the plant on their way to their own stations.

Employees also want to feel proud of their organization's role in the community. Sources of pride range from corporate participation in campaigns on behalf of charities to granting employees community work sabbaticals—as is done at IBM, Xerox and Tandem Computers, among others.

When employees have a sense of pride in their work and their company, they are more inclined to give a little extra to get the job done.

THE CUSTOMER COMES SECOND

"There is nothing we believe in more strongly than the importance of happiness in the workplace. It is absolutely the key to providing superior service. Of course our clients are the reason for our existence as a company, but to serve our clients best, we have to put our people first."

—*Hal Rosenbluth,* who has overseen the growth of his family's travel business into the fourth-largest travel agency in the United States.

Its motto? The Customer Comes Second.

 CAMARADERIE, TOO

The final factor that Levering identified as affecting the quality of the workplace is *camaraderie*: how employees relate to each other.

People want to feel acceptance, understanding, appreciation and enjoyment in their personal interactions with fellow staff. They also want access to one another's beliefs, attitudes, hopes and values. Camaraderie can have a tremendous impact on cooperation among employees. In some of the best workplaces, people claim that they are part of a "family."

Where camaraderie exists, employees feel they can be themselves, and this is especially important when the organization asks a lot of its employees. Remember the camaraderie at Southwest Airlines: Almost everyone, from baggage handlers to top executives, talks about "what a fun place it is to work" and about the love they feel toward each other and their customers. Remember

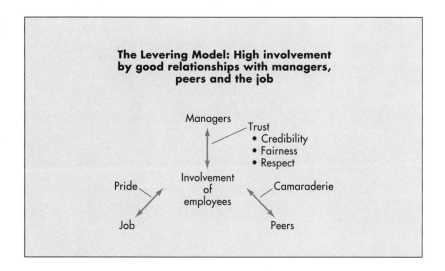

The Levering Model: High involvement by good relationships with managers, peers and the job

Managers — Trust
• Credibility
• Fairness
• Respect

Pride

Involvement of employees

Camaraderie

Job

Peers

that Southwest has been the only consistently profitable airline in the last few years, with its employees rated the most productive in the industry.

 LEVERING REFERENCE

Details of the Levering survey can be obtained from:

Great Place to Work Institute
1537 Franklin Street, Suite 208
San Francisco, CA 94109

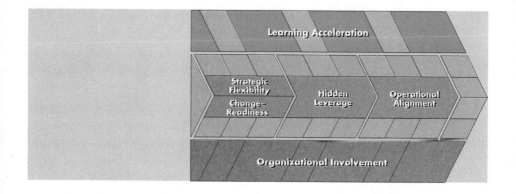

MASTER BUILDERS

Among the many forces propelling us toward the vision of a networked world is one that seems unstoppable: the use of interactive Information Technology (IT).

What we're observing now is the result of two Laws of IT. One is Moore's Law (named for Gordon Moore, a co-founder of Intel), which says that computing power and capacity doubles every 18 months as a result of developments in hardware and software. Moore's Law has held since the 1970s, although experts periodically claim that it will slow down "soon." In any case, the second law is superseding it: Metcalfe's Law, named for Bob Metcalfe, the inventor of the Ethernet standard.

Metcalfe's Law says that the benefit to users of an information network is roughly proportional to the square of the number of users. Internet, groupware and multimedia are all really in their infancy, yet already the possibilities abound.

Standing in the way of the potential benefits of interactivity from the new IT hardware and software is what the computer jocks call Wetware or Humanware—the interactions among people.

At the World Economic Forum in Davos, Switzerland, in January 1995, we were discussing where the world was going to end up when in walked John Sculley, the former head of Apple Computers. His prediction was that within 10 years we would all have access to enough technology to turn us into a "virtual community," our interactions conducted through massively sophisticated computer networks. His one great concern was that people might not be able to change their behaviors to keep pace with what the technologies made possible. We're already seeing the early stages of that problem.

Still, IBM recently bet $3.5 billion to buy Lotus, mainly to acquire Lotus Notes, the groupware technology that enables people to use their computers to work together, across organizational boundaries. IBM is betting—and Microsoft is worrying—that this technology will move the world of computer applications from its present threshold of usage to the next frontier, where the biggest potential for gains in productivity is in boosting how people work together. Lotus claims that Lotus Notes is already delivering to user companies a return on investment of, on average, about 180 percent.

 NO FRONTIERS

"A heaven of freedom, where the world has not been broken up into fragments by narrow domestic walls."

—*Rabrindanath Tagore, Nobel Prize-winning poet.*

Like Sculley, Lotus says the toughest challenges to achieving good results are not technological but psychological: the walls that people erect between themselves. Lotus discovered that to make the most of groupware technology, it's important to provide a facilitator to the people using it—not technical support, but someone who can address the interpersonal communication and collaboration issues. In other words, using IT to enable networked teams raises some major human resources (HR) issues.

We believe that is what the future holds: Human resources and information systems (IS) will be key to the future of an Accelerating Organization. At the same time, the HR and IS departments as we know them will soon be dead and buried.

How can both statements be true? Because to offer the services required of them, the HR and IS functions will have to change beyond recognition.

Over time, HR will find itself much smaller, as many of the personnel issues it historically handled become routinely handled by line managers as part of their day-to-day work. Yet some HR professionals must remain to play one of the most critical roles in the never-ending transformation of their company: They must become the full-time agents responsible for catalyzing continuous change, and creating and maintaining an infrastructure for managing people's involvement in a forever-changing organization.

The same is true of IS departments. They, too, will become decentralized into day-to-day line management responsibilities. The likelihood is that there will be little demand within the average organization for anyone who remains a pure specialist in IS. Instead, they must meld with their HR colleagues, for the IS role will also be to create and maintain an infrastructure for managing people's involvement in never-ending change. And that role is as much about people as about computers.

The two interlaced roles of the New HR and the New IS must increasingly become fully integrated, as they create the structures and mechanisms for high involvement of people. And that will no doubt be a culture shock for all the parties involved.

■ SERVING THEIR CUSTOMERS

When people in an organization know where they want to go and are committed to getting there, they need and count on timely support. In increasingly networked and team-based organizations, the principal areas in which almost every team may need support is in developing the abilities to manage the social interactions and the information technology. So HR (including Training) and IT need to be organized to provide this support to the teams.

In many companies, this comes as a revelation. Just as they are selling the notion to others in the organization that it's no longer possible for the firm to offer customers a variation of Henry Ford's any color as long as it's black, HR and IT too must be more concerned with meeting the real needs of their customers. That requires them to anticipate the types of needs their customers may have and invest in the ability to meet them flexibly and effectively.

As we've seen, the pull of magnets is more effective than repulsion alone to make change in an organization. So that's what HR, Training and IT managers should be helping their CEOs to do. And with them should be the Strategy group. Together they must help the leadership of the organization with the process of generating Pull through Vision, Strategies and Magnets. And then they must deliver the services that the teams will pull from them. Above all else, their new role is to be responsive to the teams and the leadership.

And leadership is essential.

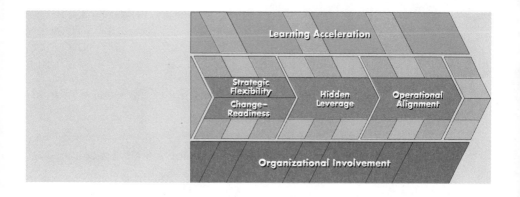

THE LEAD ARCHITECT

Lack of the right leadership may become an organization's Achilles Heel in a fast-changing, less predictable, more competitive business world.

Networked organizations place new demands on business leaders and managers: Leadership by command-and-control won't work any more. The power of ownership and hierarchical authority is simply not available in networked organizations to anywhere near the same degree it is in the traditional, monolithic corporations. Nevertheless leaders must gain the cooperation of all members of the networked organization toward the common goal.

Note that the very word *leadership*, and the way it resonates, embodies the problems many organizations are having: The word *leadership* connotes the behavior of the very few.

We believe something different, even radical: that the precepts of *leadership* are the responsibility of many people—maybe even all the people—in an organization. Of course, leadership qualities are a special requirement of top managers. But the same precepts must be manifest at all levels of a networked organization, in varying degrees.

What's more, the form in which leadership shows itself must also change. Historically leadership was largely a function of position in the hierarchy, and that can no longer be the case because the hierarchy itself is far less clear.

■ THREE PRECEPTS FOR LEADERS

Above all others, these precepts must guide the leaders of modern organizations:

Create a culture of high involvement within your organization, by setting an example and by creating effective mechanisms.

Guard the core values of your organization.

Focus above all else on people, not numbers and things.

 OWNERSHIP

"Real ownership is more than a piece of the action. It's a say in the way things are done."

—*Gordon Forward,* head of Chaparral Steel, whose workers need only 1.6 hours of labor to produce a ton of steel, compared with 2.4 hours at the mini-mills and 4.4 hours at integrated plants.

The first precept is about creating a culture within your organization of high involvement. Leaders recognize that high involvement comes from having a say in the way the business is run, very much more than through ownership of stock in the firm. So true leaders invite the involvement of everyone in improving the firm.

Good leaders set the tone, and strongly influence how others will behave by how they act. They also set up effective mechanisms that make it easy for people to get involved.

Successful multinational firms such as Nestlé and Asea Brown Boveri have developed networking mechanisms by which employees from different parts of the organization are constantly thrown together. This enables cross-fertilizing of knowledge while reinforcing the values and the trust between people in the firm. These meetings of people from different parts of the world cost money and time, but these firms don't begrudge it; rather, they consider it an essential part of their management process.

 SETTING AN EXAMPLE

Wal-Mart has grown into a $80 billion retailing giant in less than 50 years, and one of the many retailers it overtook was Kmart. The two firms looked alike, sold the same products, sought each other's customers and even dated from the same period. Now Kmart is on its knees while Wal-Mart is the second highest-performing stock in the United States (behind Southwest Airlines) from 1962 to 1992, with an appreciation of 19,807 percent.

"In the end, attitude may have made a bigger difference than strategy," Christina Duff and Bob Ortega wrote in *The Wall Street Journal* (March 24, 1995). "Mr. Walton and Mr. Glass [Mr. Walton's successor] asked their employees what wasn't working and chided them for failing to deliver any bad news. Even publicly, he and Mr. Glass were likelier to discuss Wal-Mart's weaknesses than its strengths. . . .

By contrast, Mr. Antonini [CEO of Kmart] didn't think others could tell him much about the business. He bristled at criticism and was known as the Teflon Boss because suggestions for change slid right off."

The second precept of modern organizational leadership is about guarding the core values of your organization. Providing some security is essential in organizations that are changing and adapting.

Almost everyone, you hope, is acting like a trapeze artist, letting go from one swing and trusting someone on the other swing to catch them. Often, in networked organizations, they can't even see the other person. So trust is vital, but so is some form of safety net, and core values fill that role.

 ## CREATING EFFECTIVE MECHANISMS

"What General Electric is trying to do is to create an environment in which each individual can make a connection between what he or she does each day and winning in the marketplace. When workers accustomed to being ignored see their views accepted—not just with patronizing nods but welcomed and, above all, implemented—ideas and views come in a torrent."

—*Lawrence Bossidy* (current CEO of Allied Signal), in May 1991, while he was Vice Chairman of GE.

Networked organizations will be built fundamentally on the knowledge of the values by which people will act under all circumstances. Top managers must ensure cohesion but cannot control from the center, so they must nurture and enforce core values. And those values are strongest when they allow no exception.

So though "values" sounds soft, in practice it makes for tough talk. Often it means trading something tangible, measurable and oh-so-financial for something nebulous—as Johnson & Johnson quickly did in the Tylenol crisis. These are the calls that leaders have to make, and often they must be truly courageous to make them.

 ## YOUR RESULTS ARE GREAT—YOU'VE GOT TO GO!

The general manager of the best-performing division in a large engineering company was an outstanding engineer and a hard-driving manager. But he was abusive to colleagues, and people in his division lived in fear of his tirades. He didn't trust them; they didn't trust him.

One day, the CEO called and said: "I've explained to you more than once that I want a company in which people can work effectively together, and trust each other, and not have to watch their backs all the time. You are an awful example of exactly what we must not accept of any person in this company. And because you are in such a responsible position, I have to ask you to leave."

With that, enthusiasm replaced fear on the faces of people in the division. With the clear affirmation of the corporate values, teamwork improved and the division's performance shot ahead even more.

The third precept of modern organizational leadership is the need to focus above all else on people. This is, truly, the fundamental difference between managing and leading.

Leadership has to be about people. You can manage machines, money, even complex work processes, without having to manage or lead another person. But leadership, at its heart, is a relationship with other people. Leadership is about the Human Face of Change.

 ## WEST POINT

Consider what cadets at West Point are taught about leadership. Col. Larry Donnithorne (Ret.), in "The West Point Way of Leadership" (Currency Doubleday, 1993), made his first and most important lesson this: The job of the leader is to be absolutely trustworthy and to put the needs of others first, most particularly ahead of personal considerations. Charismatic leadership is, in his book, an oxymoron—ego-driven and self-inflated, putting the self ahead of the organization's values.

West Point's second lesson about leadership is that it is not about giving orders and knowing that they will be followed. Rather, it's about honoring feelings, most particularly the feelings of your subordinates. It's about the "soft stuff," values and morals; it's about trust to build teamwork.

So organizational involvement requires more than just an understanding of network architectures and teams. It needs more than just alignment of all the policies, procedures, information systems and training courses. It demands trust. And that trust will only be nurtured by leadership throughout the organization—leadership focused on people. That will be an exhilarating challenge for many, a disturbing one for others.

A large number of top managers are not very good people-persons. Usually they are excellent at delivering performance, which is how they climbed to the top. And when such managers retire, they are often replaced by others who are fixated on the bottom line and who manage rather than lead.

That approach is no longer sustainable. Managing for organizational involvement is explicitly rooted in people and in humanity. It may also be the way of managing that is of most immediate importance to the leaders of tomorrow.

SIGNPOSTS TO MANAGING FOR ORGANIZATIONAL INVOLVEMENT

Here are some blueprints as you build a new architecture:

1. The more complex the organizational structure, the more flexible the management approach must be.

2. In place of the rigid and outmoded Master-Servant model for a business hierarchy, create a "fan" structure, with fairly rigid spokes organizing the business and more flexible links connecting them, or a "web" of intersecting and flexible links in many directions.

3. Create a team atmosphere and a team operating environment.

4. Be sensitive to people's wariness about being on networked teams. Do not impose a vision of networked teams, but let it emerge from discussions of what changes are needed.

5. Develop performance measures that support a team structure, then find reward systems that reinforce them.

6. Draw on the principles of hidden leverage. Determine the most important motivators and develop triggers tied to them. Remember that job security, challenging work and respect are often more important than financial reward.

7. Building trust is essential and relies on three factors:

   • Management must have credibility with employees.

   • Employees want a level playing field and a fair reward system.

   • Employees must feel they are respected and that their ideas get fair hearing.

8. Employees want to take pride in their work and their company., and feel a sense of camaraderie with their colleagures

9. A networked organization places new demands on leaders. It is essential to set an example for others, to guard the organization's core values and to focus above all else on people.

Learning Acceleration

Strategic
Flexibility

Change–
Readiness

Hidden
Leverage

Operational
Alignment

Organizational Involvement

MANAGING FOR LEARNING ACCELERATION

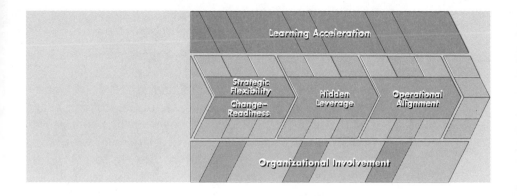

DYNAMIC GROWTH

Modern organizations face changes that are less predictable and faster than ever before: Stakeholder needs can change suddenly, competition can spring out from unexpected sources and with unanticipated vigor, the very bases of competition themselves can change. The succession of those sorts of changes creates a series of mountain ridges that modern organizations have to be able to soar above in order to survive, let alone grow.

The old trajectory of corporate flight embodied steady improvement, year after year, but that is no longer good enough. By the time organizations recognize an external change, they may not be able to react fast enough to clear the emerging hurdle, however hard they try. That was what happened to IBM when it encountered the networked PCs challenge.

To change and improve faster, organizations need the ability to accelerate their performance improvement—to improve the rate of climb. How can they do it?

■ A BALANCED SCORE CARD

For a start, change programs need to be refocused: Change must result not just in improvements in operating results but improvement in an organization's ability to improve and grow. The outcomes of such truly transformational programs are determined not just by traditional measures such as their impact on cost, quality, throughput and service time, but also by measures relating to the rate of improvement and to the organization's ability to change and respond.

Unfortunately such measures have tended to be conspicuously absent from many reengineering initiatives of the last five years and, as a result, people often focused only on short-to-medium-term benefits, rather than on sustainability and accelerated growth.

An organization that has the ability to flex, to learn and to change rapidly would be markedly different from its competitors, and both external observers and those inside would be well aware of those differences. Indeed, a measure of the success of a transformational change process would be increasing evidence of these differences.

So we must know what to look for—and we must look for it.

Earlier (in Chapter 4, Managing for Operational Alignment) we suggested the need for a balanced scorecard of change measures. So let's see what measures would be included in the score card for a process of transformational change.

From these sorts of measures you can see that an organization able to accelerate its performance improvement will feel like a

A balanced score card for a transformational change process must include measures of the organization's ability to improve

	Change in-process measures (leading indicators)	Change process outcomes (lagging indicators)
External view (observers)	For example: Curiosity about emerging needs of all stakeholders Willingness to learn from other organizations	For example: Increased pace of improvement Innovation rate of successful products and services
Internal view (participants)	For example: Availability and usage of knowledge across firm Level of experimentation throughout firm	For example: Faster rate of learning Degree to which past mistakes are repeated

very different kind of organization to work for than a run-of-the-mill company. For example, the organization as a whole will learn from experience, so that mistakes are rarely repeated. There will be a curiosity to learn. Knowledge will be shared widely, and little complacency will be evident. People will be trying to do better.

■ ORGANIZATIONAL LEARNING

These kinds of behavior are what organizational learning is all about. A useful definition, we find, is: Organizational learning is the creation, adaptation, or replication of knowledge by an organization to improve its performance.

Realizing the importance of knowledge in their organizations, a few pioneering companies—including Dow Chemical (in the United States), Skandia (the Swedish insurance company) and Canadian Imperial Bank of Commerce—have created special executive positions to focus everyone's attention on organizational learning. These posts have titles such as Director of Intellectual Asset Management, and they carry the responsibility of measuring the value of knowledge in the firm and of developing ways to increase that value by improving the "knowledge acquisition" or "learning" processes of the organization.

A fine concept. But how do we recognize organizational learning when we see it? It's really a question of looking for evidence around the types of performance measures we just ran through—measures of how the firm is transforming.

But why bother? And how could we improve it if we wanted to? That is what this section of the book will discuss.

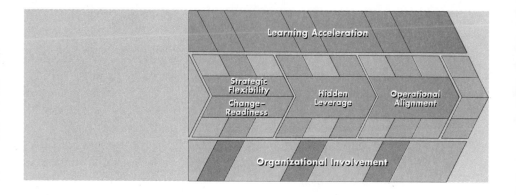

HARVESTING BENEFITS

Traditionally, the principal benefits of globalization were considered to be the optimization of the costs of production and access to additional markets for products. Now the leaders of many large companies are suggesting that the principal advantage of being a large, global organization is the greater opportunities to learn how to do things differently: The variety of environments in which large organizations operate create rich pools of knowledge that they can leverage to improve performance.

Nissan's executive vice president, Yoshikazu Kawana, says his firm wants to use the entire world as a knowledge base.

 ## ASEA BROWN BOVERI

"Our most important strength is that we have 25 factories around the world making power transformers. These people are working on the same problems and opportunities day after day, year after year, and learning a tremendous amount. We want to create a process of continuous expertise transfer. If we do, that's a source of advantage none of our rivals can match."

—*Sane Karlsson, vice president, Asea Brown Boveri,*
Harvard Business Review *(March-April 1991)*

Electrolux has a research laboratory in Finland, a development center in Sweden and a design group in Italy. Nestlé sets up internal conferences, arranges short visits and rotates key personnel among its technical and research centers around the world. Nynex, an American telecommunications company, is using state-of-the-art cabling techniques in Thailand in the hope of drawing on that experience when it comes to cabling its home market in the United States.

Multinationals are able to do extensive internal benchmarking, which can be even more potent than external benchmarking because all the information needed is readily accessible. So ABB has performance data on its 4,500 profit centers worldwide and that data is available to all its units through its Abacus information system.

But if this focus on organizational learning is changing the attitudes of leading firms about the benefits of being global, what then of the benefits of alliances and acquisition?

Historically, the purpose of alliances and acquisitions has been to optimize use of development, production and distribution assets, or to increase access to markets. The important skill for choosing good alliances and acquisitions was assessing the attractiveness and fit of assets. And the important skill for making the alliance or acquisition successful was the elimination of duplication as quickly as possible.

But many firms in many industries, particularly Japanese firms, have come from way behind to overtake their competitors in the last 25 years by using their alliances most effectively as learning opportunities.

These organizations emphasized the acquisition of knowledge as much as, or more than, the immediate improvements to the balance sheet. In a study in the Harvard Business Review (Prahalad, Hamel and Doz, Jan.–Feb. 1989) of the internal workings of 15 strategic alliances around the world, it was found that "in every case in which a Japanese company emerged from an alliance stronger than its Western partner, the Japanese company had made a greater effort to learn." NEC, for example, used a series of collaborative ventures to enhance its technology and product competencies and emerged as the only company in the world with a leading position in telecommunications, computers and semiconductors. The Western companies in their study, these authors observed, "often entered alliances to avoid investments and were more interested in reducing costs and the risks of entering new businesses than in acquiring new skills."

LEARNING FROM ALLIANCES

Honda was the first Japanese auto manufacturer to enter into an alliance with a European company to produce cars in Europe, when it joined with Rover in the United Kingdom. Rover had a history of producing good luxury cars but was struggling with poor manufacturing quality and abysmal productivity (as were almost all the once-proud British automobile firms). Honda produced excellent small cars and ran very efficient manufacturing operations. Rover needed cash; Honda wanted access to the British and European markets. So Honda invested in Rover and began producing its small cars in Britain.

This marriage produced striking strategic benefits: Honda wanted Rover's explicit and tacit knowledge of what luxury car buyers really expected, so it could move upmarket; Rover wanted Honda's explicit and tacit knowledge about efficient, high-quality manufacturing. Both parties were clear about their knowledge requirements and purposefully went about learning what they needed from each other.

Honda learned very well, developing the Legend sedan in collaboration with Rover, which Honda then sold as the Acura, a luxury-car marketing channel it established in the United States. That made Honda the first Japanese car company to move into the luxury car market in the United States, ahead of Toyota's Lexus and Nissan's Infiniti, even though Honda had no previous history of producing large cars, as Toyota and Nissan did in Japan.

And Rover, too, met its learning goals. Manufacturing productivity and quality improved remarkably as Rover engineers picked up the knowledge of Honda.

Organizational learning seems to provide satisfied shareholders, satisfied customers and satisfied employees.

For shareholders, it increases value, and that should be a good enough motivation for any hard-nosed CEO. In 1990, for example, McCaw Cellular Communications paid almost $4 billion to acquire 42 percent of Lin Broadcasting, a sum more than 17 times the book value of the net assets acquired. And that deal was just the latest in a spate of such takeovers: RJR Holdings acquired RJR Nabisco for more than $25 billion, although the book value of what it got was about $5 billion. Bristol-Myers acquired Squibb for more than $12 billion, despite the book value of little more than $1 billion. Time Inc. paid almost six times the book value to acquire 50.6 percent of Warner Communications. Eastman Kodak acquired Sterling Drug for more than four times its book value. Philip Morris got Kraft for more than five times book value. And so on.

In each case, the acquiring company believed that it was buying access to knowledge of products, markets, distribution, technologies and customers. Knowledge has become such a key resource in corporations that it is often far more valuable than the hard resources of buildings, plant, equipment, raw materials and inventory, to which traditional accounting systems assign value on the balance sheet.

Consider that the market value of the top 200 businesses on the London Stock Exchange is on average three times the worth of their fixed assets. For high-tech high fliers, it's 20 times. The same pattern is true in the United States. Some knowledge-intensive firms such as Microsoft have market values several hundred times higher than the book value of their net assets. The market has a way of recognizing the true value of organizations, even if it can't be seen from the traditional accounting perspective.

True, it's almost always easier to get a dollar of profit growth from cutting costs than from raising revenues. But investors, the final arbiters of value, well know that those two forms of profit are very different in what they portend for the companies in question. A study of 847 big public corporations by Mercer Management Consulting in Boston neatly quantifies the difference. It found that the compound annual growth rate in the market value of the companies that achieved higher-than-average profit growth but lower revenue growth than their industry's average—in other words, the cost cutters—was 11.6 percent from 1989 to 1992. By contrast, the companies that achieved higher-than-average revenue growth saw their market value jump at an annual rate double that—23.5 percent.

CUT TO GROW

"The people who go through restructuring and downsizing without a plan for growth are like the people who consume assets rather than invest in them."

—*Roger Enrico, vice chairman of Pepsico,* Fortune *(March 7, 1994).*

Unlike raising profits by shrinking the denominator of expenses, enlarging the numerator of revenue through innovation or geographical expansion requires these days a reasonable level of organizational learning: Managers need to have a vision of where technology is going, how markets can be developed, what consumers will want, where their industry is moving and how to move with it—or ahead of it.

Regrettably the restructuring era hasn't been a breeding ground for such skills. So now, managers have to learn to manage change in their organizations in ways that enhance the organization's ability to learn, to improve and thereby to grow. Otherwise they will stifle their organization's ability to compete in the future.

For customers, the extent to which organizational learning provides satisfaction is clear from the increased revenues and growth that come from a company sharpening its insights into emerging customer needs and by improving its ability to meet those needs.

Finally, for employees, the benefit of organizational learning is that it provides people more opportunities to fulfill themselves than they find in organizations that do not learn and grow. But even hard-nosed managers can reassure themselves that even this concern for employees carries a financial benefit. We have already noted (in Chapter 5) the strong correlation between Great Places to Work and sustained financial performance.

That threefold enhancement of financial performance from improved organizational learning—increased shareholder value, profitably growing revenues from satisfied customers, and increased ability and motivation of employees—should be reason enough for any CEO to take heed.

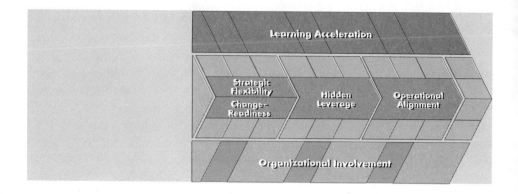

THE LEARNING FIELD

Remember our definition of organizational learning: the creation, adaptation or replication of knowledge by an organization to improve its performance. By creating knowledge, adapting knowledge that exists within the organization or is imported from outside, or simply by replicating knowledge without any modification, a company can learn.

Organizations typically view learning a lot more narrowly than they could. Organizational learning actually needs to take place in many different parts of an organization and on many different subjects. We find it helpful to place the major different forms of organizational learning into what we call a Learning Field, a matrix.

Along one dimension, we describe who is learning. The most helpful breakdown we've found is to split this dimension into four types: individual learning; team learning; learning by larger groups of people that make up an organization, and community learning, which cuts across the boundaries of a firm or stand-alone division.

The forces of competition and the nature of collaboration required among the constituents in each of these entities is different. A team within a division, for example, could be working toward a singular goal and be governed by uniform policies and incentives, while a group working across the boundaries of firms might find reconciliation of objectives to be difficult.

Undoubtedly, there is overlap in the learning that takes place in these four entities: If teams learn, so do the individuals on the teams (and, of course, teams can't learn if the members of the team don't learn). But the gathering of a bunch of knowledgeable individuals into a group does not automatically lead to collective action—just ask any elected official who emerges from a legislative debate. There's an important process of shared learning leading to alignment toward action that's required to make an effectively performing team.

So an Accelerating Organization has to address the specific needs for learning of all four entities. It cannot assume that large investments in the education and training of individual employees will create effective organizational learning, nor that it can ignore the need to invest in individual learning and growth. In addition to individual learning, it must support team learning and also the processes of learning across teams and organizations.

Along the vertical dimension, we have what the learning is about. At the bottom is learning about procedures, the details of what it takes to do something right. Much of this is explicit, simply following a step-by-step procedure, again and again. But experienced workers add to this judgments based on their experi-

The field of learning

What the learning is about	Who is learning			
	Individual	Team	Organization	Community
Vision				↑
Mental model			↑	↑
Business process		↑	B	C
Procedure	A			

ence. This is tacit knowledge. The goal of computer-based Expert Systems is to make more of such tacit knowledge explicit and the biggest hurdle has been the "knowledge engineering" required to extract the tacit knowledge from the experts in the first place.

On the next level, we have learning at the process level. We now go beyond the procedure to a collection of procedures. The more procedures being interwoven, the greater the tacit knowledge involved. Unfortunately the attitudes in most organizations still bear the legacy of the 1920s, when industrial engineers believed they could transform all necessary tacit knowledge into explicit procedures that could be assigned to individuals to implement, often mindlessly.

Many recent reengineering programs have similarly been based on the assumption that a process is merely a collection of procedures—just a very complex procedure, really. But that mental model downplays the importance of tacit knowledge in running today's organizations. It's not just a simple mental model but a simplistic one.

And mental modeling, of course, is the next level in the Field of Learning. Here we consider the learning that occurs about what the essence of a process is, and what really makes it work. Which model is chosen heavily influences the range of different processes and procedures that are then appropriate. To rethink a process rather than redesign one begins with an examination of the underlying mental model—in other words, the way you fundamentally think about things.

New mental models are difficult to learn, largely because the old ones are so difficult to unlearn, so deeply ingrained are they in your psyche. Yet the greatest opportunities for performance breakthroughs lie in learning at the level of mental models (or paradigms, as they are also called).

Closely associated with mental models is the final item on this dimension—our old motivator, Vision. The motivation for letting go of an established way of thinking, of being open to a new way, is created by an aspiration that springs as much from the heart as from the mind.

Consider what might seem an unlikely example for a corporate manager: You want to create a garden that the blind can enjoy. Your vision would undoubtedly include a garden notable not so much for its beauty as for its fragrances, sounds of water, birds, rustling reeds, the taste of certain leaves, the feel of moss on bare feet. You could do this without vision—but not without Vision.

But new visions and new mental models do not by themselves create improved performance. That can occur only when they're expressed in new designs of processes, and the processes are translated into action by the execution of procedures, whether tacit or explicit. We saw how this learning flows from vision through to operationalizing the vision when we went through the phases of managing for strategic flexibility, change readiness, hidden leverage and operational alignment.

Sometimes improvement at one level is blocked because learning is needed first at a higher level in the Learning Field. If you look back at the diagram of the field of learning, you'll find three examples of this.

Example A is a manufacturing team designing quality control procedures. In practice, the team can only design suitable procedures if it understands the process into which the quality control procedures must fit. If the manufacturing process has to be highly responsive, without in-process inventories, then it's no good designing procedures that require parts to be taken off the line for inspection while the batch from which they were taken is held up until it receives quality clearance.

Example B is a professional services firm designing a product development process. The design of process must be consistent with the firm's mental model of managing the business. If the model is of self-governing units measured principally by their bottom line, then a product development process that requires the units to share resources across their boundaries for future benefit will rapidly prove dysfunctional. The firm has either to learn a new mental model of managing the business or learn a new process of product development that fits its current mental model.

The final example, C, is a network of firms in the health-care industry that are designing a service delivery process that cuts across their firms' boundaries. They may have to begin with a shared vision of what good service may mean to customers in the future. That, in turn, may require them to rethink their mental models of what their own businesses are about, and therefore how they should manage them.

Within this Learning Field, a number of useful tools are available. That's what we'll look at next.

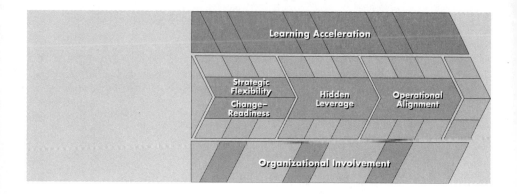

TOOLS FOR
ALL SEASONS

So far we've considered *who* is learning and *what* they are learning. Now let's look at *how* they learn. Some tools we've considered in previous parts of the book are productive conversations and scenarios to create team visions; how systems thinking and the M-E-T framework would uncover unwritten rules; and others focused on operational learning, such as the integration matrix.

Of course, there's a much larger tool kit of process reengineering techniques, such as process mapping and process breakdown analysis, and the tools of the Quality movement, which have become something of a shared language worldwide.

You can stand before a crowd of managers almost anywhere in the world, draw a Fish Bone Diagram and not have to explain what it's all about. Even 10 years ago, this wasn't the case. But Japanese companies accelerated their performance improvement greatly from the 1960s onward by involving all their employees in a process of organizational learning and improvement using these simple yet powerful learning tools. Then the rest of the world caught on.

Of the many tools available, we'd like to focus here on three, all of them particularly helpful for groups trying to select and commit to decisions, and all three of them not widely known: the *ladder of inference*, the *left-hand column* and *balancing inquiry and advocacy*.

 LEARNING TOOLS REFERENCE

A large number of learning tools, including the three we touch on here, are discussed in "The Fifth Discipline Field Book" by Peter Senge, Charlotte Roberts, Richard B. Ross, Bryan J. Smith and Art Kleiner, (Doubleday, 1994).

■ THE LADDER OF INFERENCE

Say you've been dropped off on a street corner in Manhattan to meet a colleague, James Smith. He doesn't seem to be around, but a scruffy, long-haired teenager is hanging about. He's must be unemployed if he's on the street at this time; probably he's using drugs and looking for someone to mug. You see him sizing you up, and suddenly he strides right at you, his cruel eyes locked onto yours.

Just as you're about to flinch, he says: "I'm frightfully sorry," in an impeccable English accent. "Are you by any chance waiting for James Smith?"

You nod dumbly.

"Great! I'm his son. I'm afraid he's been delayed and didn't know how to get a message to you. So he asked if I'd come and explain."

The ladder of inference

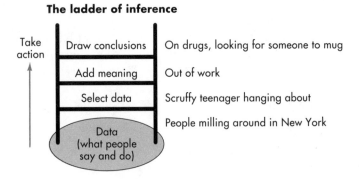

You've just been up a ladder of inference—and rapidly down it again. The ladder illustrates an automatic, unconscious process that occurs when we interact with others. It's the leaps of logic we go through in our thinking, often without being aware of them.

We jump up rung after rung very quickly; an extraordinary ability of the human brain is to select what is likely to be important and to filter out the rest. The brain's filtering mechanism is the only way we all avoid information overload. What's more, as soon as our brain selects what it will treat as important, it adds meaning and draws conclusions. All of this is heavily influenced by our beliefs, assumptions, personal values and mental models. Our thinking is effortless, fast, routine. But there's a danger, as we've seen: Our conclusions appear so obvious that we rarely bother to think about the leaps of logic we've taken to get there. And that can bring us to an inaccurate conclusion.

Remember, if you can so readily jump up a ladder of inference without stopping to reflect, so can your colleagues. And they may bring different mental models to bear and so reach different conclusions. Because they see their conclusions as obvious, they don't bother to illuminate their logic any more than you do.

The result? People who disagree often hurl conclusions at each other from the tops of their respective ladders. So when the temperature in a meeting starts rising from such activity, it's a good idea for everyone to remember that all inference is vulnerable to error.

The best ways we've found of using the ladder of inference are:

First, be more conscious of the leaps of logic you make as you climb the ladder.

Second, be far more open about that logic in a meeting, sharing the inferences you've made that led you to a particular conclusion.

Third, ask people just what led them to a particular conclusion.

When everyone in the room knows the concept of the ladder of inference, a healthy way to call "time out" is to ask what the reasoning behind a particular point is. The ladder can then be used as a way to track back to the original data that sparked the conclusion to which you took issue.

The fact that you're applying the ladder doesn't have to be made explicit; it can simply be a framework that guides you to test assumptions. (We've also been in a meeting where someone drew the whole discussion to a temporary halt with the words: "Hey, what ladder of inference did you just shoot up?")

▦ THE LEFT-HAND COLUMN

This is an exercise designed to help you become more aware of the tacit assumptions you made during what turned into a frustrating conversation. The goal is to enable you to communicate those tacit assumptions more effectively in any follow-up meeting. Alternatively you can use the exercise as a way to prepare for what you expect to be a frustrating meeting.

It's a very simple technique.

You create two columns on a piece of paper or on your word processor, and head the left-hand column "What I was thinking" and the right-hand column "What was actually said." Then you write out the conversation in the right-hand column as best as you can remember it (or as you imagine it will go), just like jotting down a film script.

Now back to the top, where you start filling in the left-hand column with what you were thinking but not saying. And that's it.

The exercise is surprisingly powerful. Merely writing out the left-hand column can illuminate aspects of your thinking that you were not aware off. Studying the overall conversation, spoken and unspoken, can be a very helpful means of preparing for a follow-up meeting.

But some words of caution: The reasons why you didn't say some things may have been valid, and it might be quite inappropriate to say them in the follow-up. It can be very tempting, after you've gone through some soul-searching, to psyche yourself up to share with someone the heartfelt concerns you have about him. But don't be surprised if he or she gets resentful if you try, and any opportunity for learning will be lost.

That is even more true if the left-hand exercise has been conducted by a group that then turns on one of its members and publicly pulls her or him to pieces. So it's clearly a matter of style and sensitivity. Sharing the contents of a left-hand column exercise with the other party can be an immensely constructive learning experience. Or it can be as destructive as they come.

It's certainly a sure sign of an advanced culture of organizational learning when a left-hand column exercise can be shared. But even just as a personal learning tool whose output isn't shared with anyone, the exercise is well worth the time.

■ BALANCING ADVOCACY AND INQUIRY

The technique of laying out your reasoning then encouraging others to challenge it is called *balancing advocacy and inquiry*. As we discussed when considering how to manage for strategic flexibility, most Western managers are preconditioned to giving their opinions, discussing facts and data of interest to them and making their needs known. This is *advocating*. Far less common is *inquiring*: genuinely exploring others' mental models to understand their lines of reasoning, asking questions, seeking clarification, looking for information, testing generalizations or conclusions— whose ever they are.

Neither hard-nosed advocacy nor soft-hearted inquiry is the ideal style for communicating with colleagues. As ever, you need a Middle Way.

Both styles have their place. Advocacy skills can often be improved simply by making more explicit your journey up a ladder of inference and then testing the result: X seems highly relevant to me. I assume Y, and therefore my conclusion is Z. Does that make sense?

Inquiry is really the mirror image of advocacy: You ask others to make their ladders of inference clearer and then test their assumptions against your own. This can often be sufficient to resolve points of contention. Should the conversation remain frustrating, use the left-hand column to clarify your concerns.

Tools such as these help to improve learning. Learning leads to knowledge, an asset that individuals and organizations can apply to produce results. So let's now see how learning leads to creation and application of knowledge.

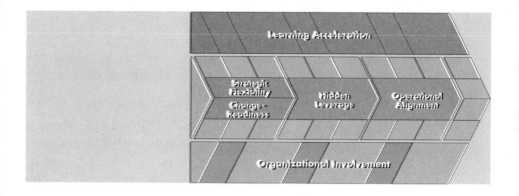

ROOTS OF LEARNING

Knowledge, fundamentally, is of two types: tacit and explicit. Understanding that can help us understand how knowledge can be created, adapted, or replicated to improve performance—in other words, the processes of organizational learning.

If we might return to the gardening metaphor: A gardening book is full of explicit knowledge. What happens when the book is published and other people read it?

It depends. A reader who learns how the nitrogen cycle works, for example, or the Latin name for a flower, is only replicating the explicit knowledge in the book. When that happens, there has been a transfer of explicit knowledge—the first learning process. The normal mechanism for such explicit knowledge transfer is teaching.

Someone who reads how to pot a cutting, and then practices with real pots, real compost and real cuttings, can rapidly internalize the explicit knowledge and develop a tacit skill. In this case, there has been an adaptation or a conversion of knowledge, from explicit to tacit—the second learning process. Under these circumstances, the book is acting as a training manual.

Some gardening skills, such as laying out a garden, are difficult to make explicit and usually remain tacit knowledge. The best way of transferring such knowledge is not by trying to make it explicit, but by getting an expert gardener to serve as coach. This is tacit knowledge-sharing—another form of replication, similar to book publishing but this time in the tacit dimension. That is the third type of learning process.

How do gardening books get written? The fourth learning process is knowledge adaptation from tacit to explicit, a vital step if the tacit knowledge of the gardener is not to remain locked in his head or only shared with a small number of friends or colleagues. Codification of tacit knowledge is achieved by systematizing that knowledge.

These four learning processes—explicit to explicit, explicit to tacit, tacit to tacit, and tacit to explicit—represent the four basic replicating-adapting learning processes.

The four replication-adaptation learning processes

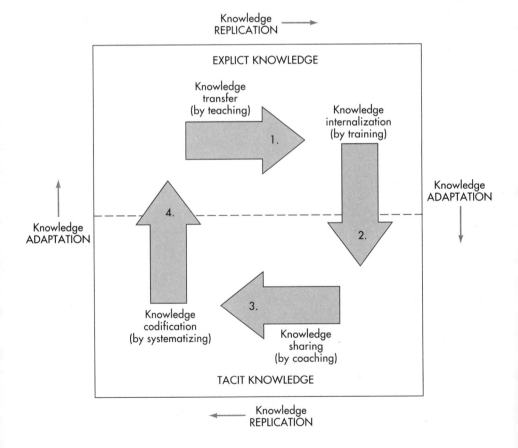

TACIT AND EXPLICIT KNOWLEDGE REFERENCE

A variant of this is in: "The Knowledge Creating Company," by Iku-jiro Nonaka and Hirotaka Takeuchi (New York: Oxford University Press, 1995).

First, there's the explicit transfer of knowledge, as when a reader digests a book full of explicit knowledge. The processes for sharing explicit knowledge are where most organizations begin their quest for becoming a learning organization—and, too often, seem to end.

Sharing explicit knowledge is the purpose of books, micro-fiches, databases, CD-ROMs and other information systems intended to make knowledge accessible to members of an organization. Usually this knowledge is the domain of the IT specialist and the librarian.

No doubt there is immense value in the availability of timely information to those who may need it. It enables them to solve problems more quickly and effectively and also improves overall organizational efficiency by reducing the time people would spend in recreating knowledge that already exists in the organization.

Yet explicit knowledge transfer should mean more than just knowledge availability. What we do not want is that traditional description of teaching by lecturing: "A process by which ideas go from the notes of the lecturer to the notes of the student without going through the mind of either."

 ## A GOOD TEACHING RECORD

At one of our clients, a teacher of safety procedures once found that a one-hour lecture he was scheduled to give clashed with an emergency management meeting he had to attend. So he told the safety class of his problem and his solution: He had tape-recorded his lecture, so he would play it for them while he went to the management meeting. He promised to return by the end of the tape for questions. So he pressed the Play button and ran out.

Fifty-five minutes later, breathless, he burst back into the classroom. It was empty, but on every desk was a small dictation machine whirring away, recording every word.

Second, someone who reads a book can rapidly internalize the explicit knowledge and develop a tacit skill. In this case, there's an adaptation or conversion of knowledge, from explicit to tacit. Internalizing explicit knowledge as tacit knowledge—the second learning process—is the essential part of individual, team, or organizational training, and application is critical. If you've ever tried learning how to use a computer by reading the manual without the computer in front of you, you know it doesn't work in the abstract. The need to act may create an interest to learn; but the process of application internalizes the knowledge. That's why Just-in-Time and Task-Aligned training (discussed in Chapter 2) work so well.

Third, some skills—such as writing poetry or playing goalkeeper on a soccer or hockey team—are difficult to make explicit; they usually remain tacit knowledge. The best way of transferring such knowledge is by getting an expert coach. This is tacit-knowledge sharing, similar to book publishing but in the tacit dimension.

Sharing tacit knowledge is achieved when people work and think together; that's how apprentices have always learned from the masters of their crafts. And that's why socializing—practice meetings, jamborees and so on—are considered essential by many firms.

DEVELOPING A TACIT UNDERSTANDING

Two professional firms recognized when they merged that they needed to pool their knowledge. They soon discovered that what each had available in documented form was only a fraction of what they could offer each other.

The only way to communicate the tacit knowledge was through shared experiences, they decided. So they selected several assignments into which they put people from both firms and asked them to reflect on what they were learning from the experience. Most everyone reported a remarkable amount of learning in a very quick time. Each discovered valuable explicit knowledge that the other firm had, but had not realized was of value to their new colleagues. Because neither firm knew what the other's collective knowledge was, it could not know what gaps its staff could helpfully fill.

Each team member also realized, intermittently, what mental models the other company used. Only by seeing how the concepts played out in practice did people appreciate their value and what they were about. And the process of shared reflection allowed each firm to make explicit for the first time just what they knew and were good at.

Fourth, knowledge adaptation from tacit to explicit is achieved by *systematizing* that knowledge. This often takes the form of writing something down in a form that people can understand, including software that displays raw data in graphical forms.

These four learning processes are not the only kinds of learning. There are also two broad kinds of learning processes through which knowledge is created: *refinement* and *breakthrough*. Both occur in the tacit domain, but often with inputs of explicit knowledge.

Refinement comes from frequent execution of a task: keyboard skills, manufacturing efficiency, adeptness at productive conversations. The goal is fixed; the approach improves. In contrast, breakthrough is an act of innovation. By definition, the goal is unknown except in broad conceptual terms.

Let's look at those more closely.

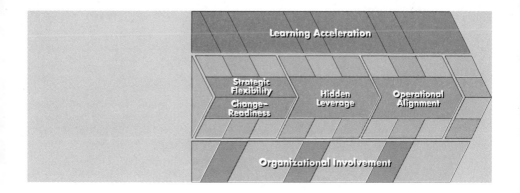

Learning Acceleration

Strategic Flexibility
Change-Readiness

Hidden Leverage

Operational Alignment

Organizational Involvement

BREEDING NEW KNOWLEDGE

Knowledge creation takes two very different forms, *refinement* and *breakthrough*. The intention of refinement is the essence of many quality initiatives: Determine the needs of your stakeholders; measure those needs; analyze what you can do to meet those needs most efficiently; and finally, install the process. Indeed, it's the essence of the Deming cycle: Plan, Do, Check, Act, used as a way to structure performance improvement in Total Quality Management. The whole focus of refinement is internal efficiency and successive improvement in the form of a feedback loop.

Breakthrough, or innovation, is intended to create an outcome that can't be known at the start: a new product concept, a technological breakthrough, an innovative strategy. You can create the conditions for innovation, but you really can't define the expected outcomes any more precisely than a broad expression of desire.

If you do try to predefine them, you are likely to ignore any ideas that don't appear to be relevant to those outcomes—in the name of focus, efficiency or whatever—and as a result, reduce the possibilities of coming away with something new.

Clearly, the innovation process tends to be a lot more messy and unstructured than the other learning processes. The logic, claim those who spend their professional careers innovating, tends to jump all over the place.

THE 60,000-PRODUCT COMPANY

Producing everything from video tapes to roof covering to adhesive tape to sandpaper to Post-its, 3M is an extraordinary company, with about 60,000 products that require some sort of coating technology. Indeed, 3M may be the most innovative large company in the world: 30 percent of its revenues come from products less than four years old; soon 10 percent will come from products less that a year old.

Most R&D people at 3M spend 15 percent of their time doing whatever research or development they like. There's a very strong shared vision of innovation; almost everyone wants to create the next Post-it.

Under such circumstances, an R&D strategy can be a mixed blessing. On the one hand, it will help to keep R&D focused; on the other, it will tend to encourage people to explore—and expect to gain funding for—only those areas that have been selected as attractive. And what if the next major innovation waiting to be discovered is in an unexpected quarter?

An example of the innovation process in practice

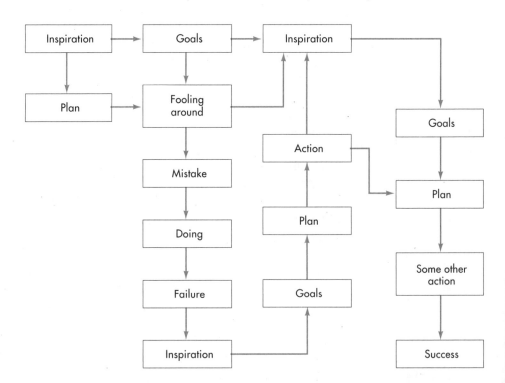

The two processes of knowledge creation

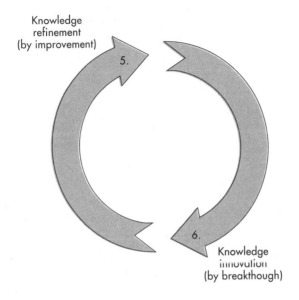

Although the context in which knowledge creation occurs is different in refinement than in innovation, both often occur together.

So we shouldn't get sidetracked into believing that a problem with fixed goals is solved only by refinement. Or that a creative problem, such as revolutionizing a product design, contains innovation but no refinement.

In practice, sparks of innovation are often followed by long periods of successive improvement. People who have worked in research labs know that the days they shout "Eureka!" are far fewer than the days they spend improving their research technique.

■ THE EDGE OF CHAOS

The anthropologist Desmond Morris noted in the 1960s that human beings are in perpetual need of both experimentation and order. Organizations are, too.

They cannot survive without changing to adapt to shifting conditions and without stability to exploit the changes they have made. Accordingly, there must always be change embedded in the stability of an organization and stability embedded in its changes.

The word *management* has acquired connotations of certainty and control. Many people assume that really good managers can be relied on to deliver on target: They're "on top of things," know what to expect, are rarely surprised. To fulfill such expectations (which they themselves often share) managers put in place structures of various forms—organizational limitations, standard procedures and the like—to reduce variations and surprises. However, the rigidity of these structures can result in an inflexibility in the organization, which cannot stay in step with the dance of change around it, and so stumbles and falls. This is a little embarrassing for the control freaks.

At the other extreme, if there were no organizational control at all, then you couldn't really say that "an organization" existed. It would have no identity whatever.

Most present mental models cannot comprehend how these seemingly opposing qualities can exist in the same system: mechanistic efficiency and organic variety, logical deduction and inductive discovery, standardization and diversity. So managers find it difficult to grasp how they could keep an organization "on the edge" between stifling order and dysfunctional chaos.

The problem is that, since Isaac Newton, scientists have pictured a world governed by regularity and order: All things are the sum of their parts; causes and effects are linked in direct, linear fashion; systems move in deterministic, predictable ways. These same principles lie beneath prevalent approaches to management: Break the organization into components and improve each, analyze problems and design logical solutions, plan precisely and control as much as possible. These principles do indeed work well when a system is largely self-contained, outcomes can be defined, and the objective is to maintain stability.

But just as these principles cannot apply to the process of innovation, they do not apply to managing enterprises in a rapidly changing world in which the organization is increasingly networked with its environment and needs to change continuously— or maybe reinvent itself.

As scientists turn their attention to systems that learn, change, and survive in competitive environments—biological, ecological and immunological systems—they are learning that these systems don't work by the Newtonian rules that apply to mechanistic systems.

Like self-learning, self-changing organisms, a company capable of creativity and novelty must find a Middle Way between chaos and stagnation. To be most innovative, it must operate on the edge of chaos, where novelty is most possible, yet without compromising the order needed to accomplish day-to-day tasks.

How can you set up the right conditions to encourage a balance between organic chaos and mechanistic stagnation? That's what we'll look at next.

 FINDING THE PAIN AT MCI

At MCI, the culture is always to flirt with the edge of chaos. MCI's founder institutionalized continuous change, saying that anyone found writing Standardized Operating Procedures would be dealt with. Now MCI is evolving backward, to create some structure in order to capture what it has learned.

Of its 37,000 employees, a small group of 50 to 60 meets quarterly to work on learning and change. They use a model of process management that is so unfixed as to be a non-model. "Find the pain and eliminate it" is MCI's simple operating principle—highly appropriate for the blinding rate of change in its industry.

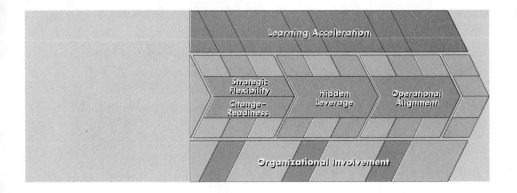

CULTIVATING A MIDDLE WAY

Managers are not alone in confronting this seemingly funda-mental problem of reconciling two opposing views of how things work.

Scientists, too, grapple with this. Often what they are working on is related to the essence of things, and it's left to business peo-ple and managers to convert the scientists' discoveries into practi-cal applications.

At the Santa Fe Institute, in New Mexico, scientists have been making some interesting discoveries. Chris Langton, for instance, discovered that to keep systems on the edge between chaos and stagnation, where they are continuously learning and rejuvenat-ing, you have to find the parameters, through experiments, at which the system stays on this edge. If the parameters drift too much one way, the system freezes; too much the other and the system disintegrates.

 COMPLEXITY THEORY REFERENCE

For a fascinating description of Langton's discovery, see M. Mitchell Waldrop's "Complexity: the Emerging Science at the Edge of Order and Chaos" (Simon & Schuster, 1992).

For organizations, the Middle Way is where the organization is on the edge between stagnation and chaos—and that is just where rapid organizational learning can occur.

Take a margarita glass—a glass with a small bowl at the bottom that opens into a larger bowl at the top. Now put a few marbles in it. Try to spin the marbles around the glass, and you'll find that if the marbles slip into the small bowl, they are difficult to move around. If they are in the larger bowl, however, they move freely. Should they climb above the rim of the glass, of course, the marbles shoot off, out of control.

An organization that gets too tightly controlled feels like the lower bowl. An organization that allows sufficient experimentation and is adequately in control—sufficiently open but bounded—is like the upper bowl of the margarita glass. It is in the middle, on the edge between stagnation and chaos.

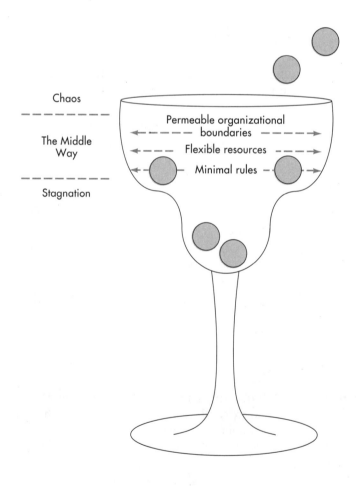

Chaos

The Middle Way

Stagnation

Permeable organizational boundaries

Flexible resources

Minimal rules

◼ FOUR CONDITIONS FOR ACCELERATED ORGANIZATIONAL LEARNING

What keeps people in organizations together in the middle of the glass, on that edge between stagnation and chaos? Tracing the history of organizations that have endured by learning and evolving, observing the experience of organizations that have introduced new ways of managing, we find four overriding conditions that need to be satisfied:

• Creative tension between shared vision and acknowledged reality
• Permeable organizational boundaries
• Flexible resource architecture
• Minimal rules

All but the first condition for accelerated learning apply conceptually to organizations of many different kinds: other biological species, even computer programs. But as far as we know, the first condition—the conscious vision of being better—applies only to human beings.

Managers have a strategic task and an operational task to get the architecture right for their organizations. The strategic task is to determine how much "experimentation" and innovation they need for success in their business, versus efficient exploitation of resources. That would depend on the business they are in and on their strategy for business success, and would determine the type of architecture they need. The operational task is to ensure that the three dimensions are aligned with respect to each other—and that all are tuned for the desired effect. For example, minimal rules and freedom to experiment are not of much use if the resources are inflexible and do not allow experimentation and change.

Of course, we've already described the importance of creating a strong shared vision and the magnetic pull of creative tension (in Chapters 1 and 2). So now we need to examine the other important structural foundations that encourage and enable all types of organizational learning processes.

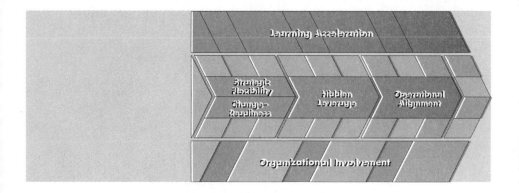

LOW HEDGES

Encouraging permeable boundaries within an organization, even encouraging people from different organizations to work together, brings two main benefits.

First, it helps move knowledge around the organization, especially tacit knowledge. Second, it leads people with different perspectives to work together, so they have a much better chance of discovering and sharing fresh insights and creating knowledge. Indeed, such "boundarylessness" was GE's way to implement its strategy to be No. 1 or 2 in every business in which it operated.

 PERMEABLE BOUNDARIES

General Mills has factories where there are no managers or supervisors present and employees function in self-directed work teams. In one such plant, employees rotate regularly between five assignments and make decisions regarding production collectively.

At J.P. Morgan, employees join work teams immediately after training. They get immediate responsibility and the freedom to approach anyone in the company for help in solving a problem.

Boundaries need to be more flexible than the typical walls between functions, business units and other organizational divisions that exist in many mechanistic organizations. They should not, however, be so vaporous as to leave people with little sense of the group or the team with which they need to adhere most closely in order to achieve organizational goals.

At many companies, job rotation among functions, regions and teams has been institutionalized, as another way of moving knowledge around, even where boundaries are fairly hard. That can help, but for two reasons it's not enough.

First, it's a very slow way of diffusing knowledge, so the knowledge may be out of date by the time it gets diffused. And second, frequent job rotation can itself lead to systemic problems for the organization, particularly chronic short-termism.

 ## LEARNING AT KAO

Kao, Japan's leading cosmetics and toiletries maker, opens many channels to increase communication and collaboration between R&D personnel across divisional lines. The previously mentioned "Knowledge Creating Company," by Nonaka and Takeuchi describes the many ways people are enabled to communicate with each other.

First, Kao has introduced "free access to information" computer systems throughout the company, through which any member, no matter what her position or to what section she belongs, has access to the full database.

Second, all divisions and functional groups within Kao are situated in large open spaces. In laboratories, for example, researchers do not have their own desks but share big tables. This fosters tacit information sharing, supplementing the explicit information shared through the computer systems.

Third, information sharing is enhanced by open meetings: all meetings, including top-management meetings, are open to all employees.

Fourth, personnel are moved around among divisions and functions in a "fluid personnel change" system.

And fifth, all change and improvement projects, whether product development or the simplification of corporate staff operations, are managed by cross-functional and cross-divisional teams.

Management consulting companies must continuously generate knowledge that is useful for their clients. The new knowledge is created by people working fluidly across organizational boundaries. Project teams include people with different disciplines, from different parts of the world and with different perspectives—all working together around a common issue. Teams form and dissolve as projects are completed and new projects have to be staffed.

In addition, people connect in "practices" or "centers of excellence" to distill and share their learning around subjects of interest to them. Yes, the counter-tug of efficiency always arises. There are pressures to keep people working within their unit boundaries and within their regions and, in the extreme, to reduce the travel and communication associated with "practice" activities rather than revenue-generating work.

But the companies know that if they slip too far down that slope and let the organizational boundaries become rigid, they will lose their knowledge-generating ability, the benefit to their clients, and their competitive position.

Whether in management consultancies or elsewhere, people are encouraged to get together across their organizational boundaries. The purpose of these get-togethers is not merely to conduct business—in fact, sometimes no business at all is on the agenda—but to "network." In other words, people are brought together to connect with people outside the unit boundaries, to build camaraderie and trust, and to enable the sharing of tacit knowledge.

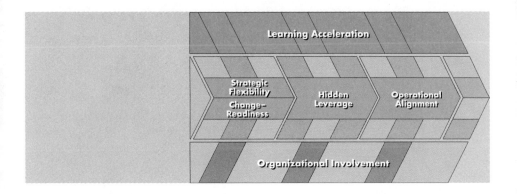

Learning Acceleration

Strategic
Flexibility

Change-
Readiness

Hidden
Leverage

Operational
Alignment

Organizational Involvement

HOTHOUSE SYSTEMS

Information managers considering the problems of improving knowledge transfer and knowledge conversion soon realize that many issues are outside the domain of conventional information systems.

Much of the knowledge in an organization is difficult to convert into a form that can be clearly documented, stored and shared. A significant proportion is tacit and reposes in the minds of people. Good knowledge databases always include the names of people to contact for more information on the subject, and so point their customers to the possibility of sharing tacit knowledge.

Unfortunately, however, the transfer of tacit knowledge is often outside the area of expertise of those skilled in information technology. And only if the tacit knowledge can be converted to explicit knowledge can the information folks put it into their databases and use their technology to make it available to everybody.

A second problem is that it's often not clear how people will, in practice, use the explicit knowledge in an information system. As a result, many information managers often don't know what is the most useful form in which to make knowledge available.

The third problem for information managers is that, even when knowledge is available in an explicit form to individuals or teams, they're often reluctant to share it with the rest of their organization. This should not really be surprising: Individuals and teams, like corporations, recognize that knowledge conveys power.

Yet despite these problems, information systems can be important aids to organizational learning. And as we've said before, in the Twenty-First Century we expect the role of the Information Technology department increasingly to meld with the role of Human Resources, and with that of Training, if Training is now a separate department. Nowhere is this consolidation more apparent than when considering information systems as an enabling technology for organizational learning.

Every day, new and exciting technologies are emerging or becoming affordable that can have a profound impact on how people capture knowledge, achieve understanding and communicate with one another. All these activities are fundamental building blocks of organizational learning. So let's run through the benefits of how information systems can sustain the six learning processes.

■ SYSTEMS FOR KNOWLEDGE REPLICATION AND ADAPTATION

Without doubt, the greatest current application of information systems is for the first learning process—transfer of explicit knowledge. Technologies that efficiently and effectively manage huge stores of data provide an important foundation for learning applications. These days, information systems are expanding beyond traditional text and graphics displays to incorporate video, photographs, sound and speech.

During the 1980s, however, information systems became more available to support the second learning process—explicit-to-tacit internalization of knowledge. While computer-based training has existed for some time, its impact was modest until it was able to capitalize on more powerful PC's, laser-disk storage, high-resolution graphics and the like.

Interactive multimedia systems immerse students in an experience, allowing them to experiment with options, make mistakes and receive feedback. A company called Interactive Video Concepts Inc., for example, has developed videodisk-based systems for training hospital social workers to assist family members dealing with someone's serious illness or death.

The system starts in a conventional videotape format, presenting the students with the type of situation they will face on the job. Then, at several points in the story it is telling, the system pauses and requires the students to make a choice from a menu of possibilities. The students get immediate feedback about the consequences of a particular action, along with comments from an instructor about the wisdom of each choice.

VIRTUAL TRAINING

Motorola's highly automated pager assembly plant in Florida employs very few staff members, and all of them must be extremely well trained. Because of the prohibitive cost of using the expensive three-shift facility for training, Motorola developed a multimedia-based training system. This interactive system has proven itself by reducing both training time and the number of mistakes made by newly trained operators.

Motorola conducted an experiment that compared the number of errors made by workers trained with the standard method to the number made by those trained with the simulator. The company found that the computer-trained users made one-sixth the number of errors of those trained traditionally.

Until recently, the third learning process—sharing of tacit knowledge—was not suited to information systems. In the 1990s, however, two advances are starting to make a difference. The first is "groupware." While it is primarily aimed at explicit knowledge-sharing, the more powerful systems make it easy for people to add their own comments, refer to conversations with customers and add intuitive reactions, which together may allow a user to infer something beyond the explicit knowledge on the system.

The second advance is virtual reality. Such systems allow the user to interact with data in a far more tacit form than conventional systems allow. Investment portfolio analysis, for example, frequently involves trying to comprehend relationships among many variables. Business investment might include such variables as: risk vs. income, investor goals and objectives for growth vs. capital conservation, income and expected trend, obligations and needs for liquidity, costs of making transactions, expected return on investments and needs to ration capital.

That's too many variables for people to hold in their heads. Users of virtual reality technology can view all the data as three-dimensional shapes, which they can actually manipulate by using a "data glove." That experience provides them with a tacit understanding of the relationships among the variables.

Some aspects of tacit-to-explicit knowledge codification—the fourth learning process—are also starting to be automated. Expert systems build on artificial intelligence technology to capture knowledge and make it available to others. Originally it was assumed that the knowledge would all be explicit.

It has become clear, however, that it is often possible to elicit knowledge, perhaps from a number of experts, that no one was previously able to convey. As a result, some knowledge encapsulated by successful expert systems is a codification of previously tacit knowledge.

Other technologies for making tacit knowledge explicit are visualization systems. Because modern data-processing frequently produces huge amounts of data, various systems have been developed to help people better understand the data—and to make more explicit a sense of what the figures imply. A simple example is the powerful graphics ability of modern spreadsheet programs. Another example is the use of geographic overlays to help in understanding data with spatial dimensions.

VITAL STATISTICS

Levi Strauss, Banc One, Arby's and Kaiser Permanente are among the companies using geographic data overlays to better understand their market dynamics. The application works almost the same way for each firm: Vital revenue statistics by product category are divided into geographic regions, in some cases down to the postal-code level. By using colors to represent income level or education, the product sales and growth can be correlated with these demographics. Using the analysis, the product mix can be adjusted to balance and maximize revenue for the firm as a whole.

SYSTEMS FOR KNOWLEDGE CREATION

Such techniques allow more than just adaptation of tacit knowledge to explicit. They help people to refine knowledge and create knowledge of how to improve something—the fifth learning

SUPERMARKET SCRUTINY

Information Resources Inc. (IRI) of Chicago has made the capture and analysis of information from supermarket optical scanners the centerpiece of its business. By going into midsized markets, IRI is able to get nearly 100 percent access to the data being captured by every supermarket in the community. It collects and analyzes this data for the market as a whole and tracks specific households whose members show bar-coded ID cards at checkout.

As product manufacturers experiment with different advertising and promotion mixes in the market, the monitoring gives them near-instant feedback into the effectiveness of each dollar spent on promotion. In some markets, the manufacturers have even employed technology to vary the advertising on a home-by-home basis and track the impact of each ad.

Similarly, such companies as Citibank analyze the purchase patterns of each Mastercard, Visa and Diner's Club customer to develop a package of coupons designed for each customer's household. Analysis of huge volumes of data like these can help companies learn about their customers' habits and preferences, which in turn helps them improve promotional campaigns.

process. So-called "data mining" systems capitalize on the evolving ability of information technology to help discover meaning and make practical sense out of masses of transaction-based data.

Even knowledge innovation—the sixth learning process—may be about to get a boost from emerging information technologies. In the past, it has been difficult to use information systems to support innovation, because they were locked into the models by which they had been programmed.

But such limitations may not apply much longer. "Neural networks," for example, are based on a fundamentally different architecture than other computers. They're similar in concept to the flexible interconnections of neurons in the brain, and as such, they are proving very promising at pattern recognition. Conventional computers, more proficient at arithmetical computations, are not so good at finding patterns. Neural nets are not programmed as other computers are, and they are able to learn to detect significant attributes of a pattern unaided. In that sense, they program themselves.

■ THE DANGERS

But we shouldn't get carried away. Although information systems will continue to bring extraordinary benefits to organizations, they also carry an insidious danger: The highly complex computer systems of today are—necessarily—based on the mental models of yesterday. So they classify all new data in ways that reinforce the existing mental models and theories. And that might prevent new knowledge from being created.

It's a similar danger to that faced by organizations that rely only on customer feedback in preformatted forms, instead of talking with customers face to face.

How dangerous can this be?

The story of the discovery of a hole in the ozone layer is illuminating. Some evidence was available, on the ground, that led scientists to hypothesize that there was a hole. So they looked for supporting evidence in computer-analyzed data from the Nimbus satellite. They sifted through five years of such analysis but found no evidence to support their hypothesis.

Fortunately, they persisted and went to the raw data that the satellite provided. And there they found their evidence. It turned out that the computer had been systematically discarding the unusual data as spurious, because its software had been programmed according to a mental model that had not allowed for such a possibility. Evidence is of little value if it's filtered through wrong assumptions.

 ### MRS. FIELDS' COOKIES

In 1977, Debbie Fields, 20 years old, began selling her home-baked cookies at a store in Palo Alto, California. By 1981, her company had 14 stores. Information systems were a critical component of the growth; her husband, Randy, was a computer enthusiast whose concept was to provide expertise directly to every store from headquarters, in order to ensure that each was run exactly the same way as Debbie had run the first.

As much as possible was automated, and interacting with customers was all that employees were left to do. By 1987, more than 300 stores produced earnings of $17.7 million on sales of $113 million. Then the market changed.

Mrs. Fields' success inspired intense competition from other cookie makers, despite a growing interest in nutrition and personal fitness with which they all had to contend. In 1988, the company experienced a loss of $18.5 million—and it never recovered. By 1993, lenders took 79 percent of the company in exchange for writing off $94 million in debt, and Debbie Fields had to step down as president and CEO.

What went wrong? Brandon Gill of Florida State University studied the rise and fall of Mrs. Fields, and concluded that the main contributor to the company's downfall was its inability to achieve organizational learning in a complex environment. A principal cause of this was the highly efficient computerized management system: The system could only scan for information it was programmed to look for. Staff in the stores had to feed back information in the formats specified: It was a hassle for them to feed back anything else.

So the information systems constrained the unstructured problem-solving needed to regain control.

The lesson? Avoid the temptation of automating your organization so heavily for productivity gains that the systems unintentionally filter the channels of communication needed for rapid organizational learning. This is particularly true of scanning the environment. Even as middle-management roles become increasingly automated, the scanning activities must be maintained with the full richness of before. And new communication channels should constantly be being opened.

TWO-WAY COMMUNICATION AT MICROSOFT

The Microsoft Developers Network, which provides technical support to software creators using Microsoft compilers and languages, makes heavy use of information systems. But it ensures a rich two-way information flow with special quick-answer phone lines, fax, E-mail, electronic bulletin boards and other media.

Information Systems managers need to challenge constantly the mental models of the past to see if they have become outmoded. Perhaps the easiest way of avoiding the trap of Silicon Stagnation is to try applying information technology only to tasks that can't be accomplished manually—rather than automating decision-making performed by people.

The same principle of avoiding rigidity applies to all the other important resources of the organization. This includes machinery and equipment and even the design of offices. Mass production systems, with dedicated special-purpose machines and tools, are highly efficient—for the relatively narrow purposes for which they are designed.

In other words, they are "frozen learning." Procedures that have been found to work most efficiently for those purposes are designed into rigid machinery and tools. The machines will keep repeating those procedures faithfully. But watch out if you want to experiment with a new procedure.

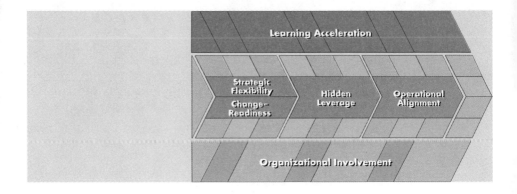

FREEDOM TO GROW

John Holland of the Santa Fe Institute has studied how systems learn new rules by which to improve their performance. Complex systems, he found, require very few rules to govern themselves and perform. More importantly, he found that the more rules a system attempts to follow, the slower it gets at improving its performance. What happens is that the system seems to get entangled in the cross-connections of the various rules.

All successful systems, it appears, including businesses, go through a process of learning better rules. A system starts with a small set of default rules to protect itself and a few plausible "strong" rules, which it believes may improve its performance. It then compares these strong rules with other potential strong rules of which it becomes aware and chooses to adopt some, or combine them with existing strong rules to create new strong rules.

Holland calls this "the cross-over process": While adopting new strong rules, a system sheds some existing rules. It then compares its new strong rules with other rules, and so on, as it keeps learning and improving. Two important principles emerge for accelerating the improvement of a system's performance:

The Freedom to Experiment: A system needs a cross-over process by which new rules can be learned.

The Ability to Unlearn: A system must let go of weak rules, so it does not get frozen from too many rules.

At some point, almost everyone has experienced the stultifying effect of excessive rules and procedures. Yet when management comes across a new rule or procedure that appears effective, its instinct is often to adopt it. Managers make the assumption that there can be no harm in having a rule or procedure for something that's worth doing anyway. And thus, many organizations build up mountains of manuals under which they bury the ability of the organization to change and learn.

 ## NEW RULES FOR OLD

A Fortune 50 consumer products company appointed a group to determine how to improve on-time deliveries of products. The team examined the entire system, found the causes of the problems and determined the changes in procedures that were needed. And it recommended those changes to management.

Management, however, demurred. Instead it asked the team to share its model of the system with department heads. The team did so, and in the process came up with a refined set of procedures to effect the improvements, which it urged management to implement immediately.

Again management demurred, this time asking the team to share its model with all operators. The team did, and by the time it had finished, it discovered something intriguing: Without management having formally announced any new procedures, on-time deliveries had increased from 40 percent to 90 percent.

A sister division in the company had the same need to improve on-time deliveries. An improvement team examined its system, found very similar causes of problems to what the other division had found—and, with confidence, recommended that similar new procedures be implemented.

This time management agreed. And unfortunately, the on-time deliveries improved much more slowly.

This contrast should not have been a surprise. In the second division, the final implementors did not determine the changes that they would have to make to operating rules and procedures. They were just informed of new rules. In the first division, the final implementors had understood what the problem was and then modified their own rules, gracefully shedding old rules as they did. In the second division, the operators were given new rules in which they did not have full confidence. So they wouldn't let go of the old rules, leaving the system cluttered.

We strongly believe that some principles are emerging for managing the formal, official rules of an organization—the "written rules"—to maximize the chances of organizational learning:

- Organizations should minimize the number of written rules they use.
- Management should specify only critical rules needed to guide the organization.
- Those who must apply new rules should develop them.
- Everyone should keep testing the rules and looking for better ones.

This "minimum critical specification" is not anarchy—quite the opposite. The few best rules are given space to have full effect, uncluttered by the often contradictory minutiae in manuals of operating procedures. Nor is the minimalism of rules management by abdication. Rather, it represents a management focus on the organization's ability to discover ever better rules.

 ## NORDSTROM'S EMPLOYEE HANDBOOK

The retailer Nordstrom has a one-paragraph employee handbook that states: "Set both your personal and professional goals high. We have great confidence in your ability to achieve them. Nordstrom Rules: Rule #1: Use your good judgment in all situations. There will be no additional rules."

Our colleagues at Arthur D. Little have applied this philosophy to some pretty down-to-earth problems, including improving the performance of manufacturing organizations in a range of industries: metals companies, chemicals companies, electronic companies.

The people responsible for performance, including the operators, jointly learn about their system, using their factory as their laboratory. They then carefully let go of rules, and controls related to those rules, that are not critical.

In every case, the results have been impressive in terms of reduction of failures, increase in yield, shorter throughput times and increased equipment utilization. In one case, a European metals product company went from a 30 percent cost disadvantage, compared with its Japanese competitors, to a 15 percent advantage.

An interesting side effect of this minimalism is the reduction of the number of controls and computers required to gather, analyze and sort data that is needed to manage the system. At the metals product company, for example, all the large computers that had been deemed indispensable for running the operations became superfluous. The few crucial rules that needed to be managed required only one PC.

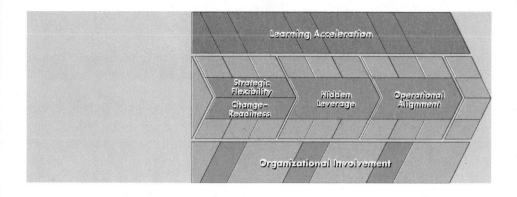

NURSERIES

We've described the critical architectural features of organizations that allow experimentation while having sufficient structural firmness to exploit the benefits of successful experiments. So let's return to the need to foster experimentation to accelerate learning and improvement.

If you want to grow a prize rose bloom, you prune your rose bush hard, reducing the number of shoots and forcing the plant to push all its energy into one or two blooms. The same is true if you hope to grow the biggest pumpkin at the fair.

You hope the weather will cooperate, and your contender will survive any unexpected turns in the weather. It's a good strategy when weather conditions are predictable, but risky if the weather is less so. And, faced with the prospect of unpredictable weather, you might choose to leave a few more shoots on the plant or pumpkins on the vine to increase the odds of success.

This horticultural model offers a lesson for organizations: Successful breakthroughs are more likely to arise when strategies for creation match external conditions. And since we've all agreed that external conditions are changing rapidly, what are the implications for modern organizations?

 ## THE UNTIDINESS OF INNOVATION

"The ordinary manager has a craving for order. The leader understands that innovation is almost always an untidy process."
—*L.W. Lehr, former CEO of 3M*

They need to encourage more experimentation so that at least some experiments have a chance of coinciding with external conditions.

John Holland finds from his computer models of self-emerging systems that only one of every five experiments is a breakthrough—but that one is good enough to make the whole system successful. This seems to confirm the principle of Vilfredo Pareto, the early Twentieth Century economist: 80 percent of the benefit comes from 20 percent of the input. (Pareto tried to name this "the law of maldistribution," but we all know it as "the 80/20 rule.")

When Pareto's principle is applied to improvement processes, the implication is that we should concentrate our efforts on only those 20 percent of the opportunities that will provide 80 percent of the benefit. And it works. Pareto's principle is one of the seven tools of quality management that were taught to all employees in Japanese companies in the 1970s and 1980s. It has also been used by people in companies elsewhere to improve quality and productivity.

Holland has studied the innovation strategies of several companies and confirmed that organizations make money on only about 20 percent of their projects. So the Pareto principle applies to the innovation process also. This revelation would lead many managers to concentrate on only 20 percent of the innovation projects. The question is: which ones?

The problem, of course, is that with an innovation process, you don't know what the outcome is going to be so you don't know which projects to cut. Only if you start out with all 100 percent can you expect that you'll end up with the winning 20 percent. If you want to increase the number of winners, you have to increase the number of experiments (and by Pareto's law, you'll need five new projects for each new success you want).

 ## GIVING THE BOOT TO BOOTLEG PROJECTS

In the 1960s, IBM had bootleg research—projects outside the official research programs—in all its labs. In the 1970s, the bootleg research was weeded out in the name of better management of R&D.

Then came the 1980s, when IBM was unable to respond to the changes in the marketplace. The culture of tightening up and buttoning down, especially when applied to areas where continuous innovation and adaptation is required, could well have been a contributory factor.

It's certainly a contrast to the enduring spirit of experimentation embodied in Honda's "Let's Gamble," Tata's "Something New From Everyone" and Chaparral Steel's "If it ain't broke, break it!"

Permission to experiment is one indication of any organization's support for learning. But it tends to be easier to fund such experimentation and turn a blind eye to it if the experiments are in an R&D laboratory. A lab, after all, is supposed to be a safe-failing space—a place with room for the errors of trial-and-error.

But what if the experiments are needed within the operations of the company—if the company has to experiment on itself, to see how it really works and to test new ideas on how it may work more effectively? That's when simulation models can serve as invaluable learning spaces, enabling managers to play "what if" learning games.

But be careful: Computer simulations should be viewed primarily as learning tools, a way to explore possible systemic connections and leverage points. They are not, in general, tools for predicting quantitative outcomes—and, in many cases, they are not even accurate in predicting qualitative outcomes.

Unless many people's tacit knowledge has been codified into a simulation, there is still no substitute for a broadly selected group of people sitting around a table, pooling their knowledge, trying to predict outcomes, then planning a safe experiment to test their conclusions.

You simply cannot make a useful simulation model for an operation unless you can describe the real-world operation in a systemic way; often no applicable model exists. So you may have to experiment with the actual operation, poking into it, to understand the systemic connections. You need a safe-failing way to do this, so that even if the experiment fails, the operation is not affected. And even then, the simulation is bound to be an approximation, maybe a gross approximation, of what is a highly complex situation.

Thus the importance of designing the organization and its processes and resource systems so that experiments can flow freely while efficiency is maintained.

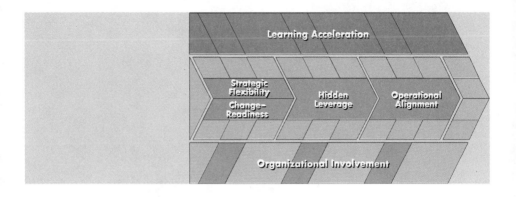

INCREASING THE YIELD

THE SIX MAIN LEARNING PROCESSES

PROCESS	TECHNIQUE	TYPE
1. Transfer	Teaching	Replication
2. Internalization	Training	Adaptation
3. Sharing	Coaching	Replication
4. Codification	Systematizing	Adaptation
5. Refinement	Improvement	Creation
6. Innovation	Breakthrough	Creation

All six learning processes we've discussed are encouraged by a creative tension between the shared vision in the organization and its current reality, and are supported by three strong roots: permeable organizational boundaries, flexible information and resource architecture, and minimal rules that allow for experimentation.

These three roots are features of the organization's structures, but the organization has to learn how to tune its own structures (much the way a sophisticated race car offers the ability to fine-tune its suspension). And as the company tunes the structures, it can improve the processes of organizational learning, and so become more adept at fine-tuning its structures. This will enhance learning. . .and that is how the organization encodes

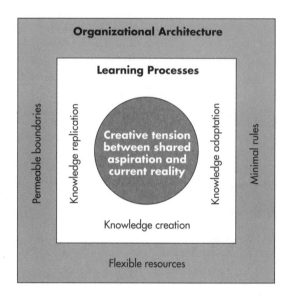

organizational learning into its DNA. That is how it can learn to change and change to learn.

In the successful organizations of the Twenty-First Century, learning processes will feed a virtuous cycle: nurturing the roots of learning, so increasing learning, providing more sustenance for its roots and further increasing their yield. In that way, organizational learning accelerates.

Visions and strategies, too, are tied into the learning cycle and are heavily dependent on the *breakthrough* and *refinement* learning processes. As the learning processes improve, so the organization will be able to create better visions and strategies, which will in turn encourage stronger learning processes, and so on.

The real lesson: Organizational learning is attractive not just because it improves the performance of an organization as a whole—but because it also improves organizational learning itself. This improves organizational performance and also improves organizational learning still further, which improves organizational performance even more. Such a learning cycle will be the core of the accelerating organizations of tomorrow.

As the cycle continues, it's important that none of the individual improvement programs work counter to the desired goal of accelerated learning. At Cemex, for example, all the cement plants described the nature of the accelerating organization they wished to be in terms of the organizational and process principles that had to apply. The company now ensures that all proposed changes, whether through a reengineering program, a new computer system or a new wage agreement with the unions, are consistent with those parameters.

Let's consider how one company flourished by turning itself into an Accelerating Organization.

In 1945, a group of executives of Krauss Mafei, the large German engineering combine, waited at the bombed-out rail station in Munich for two visitors from India, the chairman and the president of the Indian company Tata.

Krauss Mafei was shattered, its employees hungry, and during the subsequent meeting, the Germans offered the Indians the knowledge to make locomotives. Forbidden by the Allies from entering into any formal agreement with the Indian company, they said: "Take our people. They are our assets, and the repository of our knowledge. Look after them and learn what you can from them. When we can afford to have them back, we would like them to return."

Soon after, Tata formed the Tata Engineering and Locomotive Company (Telco), which manufactured steam locomotives for many years at a factory in Jamshedpur in eastern India. The German engineers helped Tata learn their craft and were generously looked after until they returned to Germany.

Another group of Germans, from Daimler Benz, came in 1954 and taught Telco about making trucks. Telco learned so well that eventually almost all the trucks' components were made by Indians to Daimler Benz standards, and Daimler Benz exported the vehicles to customers in other countries.

Thirsty for knowledge, eager to make itself the most integrated vehicle manufacturer in the world, Telco now wanted to design models of trucks—and even design and make the machines needed to make the trucks, to get to the heart of the manufacturing process. So it acquired an enormous barren plain in Pune, in western India, and there created what its chief executive officer at the time, Sumant Moolgaokar, called the Learning Factory. The first buildings were a training school and an experimental workshop, which was the nucleus of an R&D center.

Telco chose companies in Europe and in Japan that it could learn from, and made its objective the improvement of the process by which it learned technology. It decided to measure two things: how quickly it could acquire a new technology—judged by how fast it could independently replicate the products of its partners—and how thoroughly it could master the technology—judged by how quickly it could use the technology for applications that the collaborator had not provided the know-how for.

Telco also designed processes for the acquisition of the tacit knowledge that its collaborators had. It recognized early on that the technical drawings and process sheets—those repositories of explicit knowledge—were incomplete without the tacit knowledge in the minds of those who used that knowledge. So it experimented with combinations of teaching, training and coaching.

Within 15 years, that barren plain between the training center and the R&D center was buzzing with machines and workers, producing a remarkable range of trucks and engineering products. But still, Telco was not complacent. It continued to move toward its vision of an Accelerating Organization. Telco envisaged and implemented, step by step, the organization changes required to have more permeable boundaries. It changed its salary and incentive structures to enable multiskilled people to work across organizational boundaries; it converted the industrial engineering department and the reams of procedures that emanated from there into a service for teams improving their own procedures.

Every change in production equipment, computer technology and factory layout has moved the operation closer to a level of flexibility that allows rapid prototyping and experimentation with products and processes. So as the operation has grown, it has changed, and as it has changed, it has been able to grow even faster—in its knowledge, and also in its product range, its output, its productivity and its profits.

It is an extraordinary story of 50 years of organizational learning.

Let's keep in mind, though, that a fixation on organizational learning can be counterproductive. The benefits of learning acceleration simply cannot be realized without also managing for strategic flexibility, change-readiness, hidden leverage, operational alignment and organizational involvement.

Organizational learning does not—cannot—stand alone: It may drive the whole organization, but it is driven by the whole organization as well.

So where do you begin?

SIGNPOSTS TO MANAGING FOR LEARNING ACCELERATION

Want to learn how to learn? Here are some pointers:

1. Change programs need to be refocused on improving an organization's ability to improve and grow.

2. An Accelerating Organization needs to create environments for all forms of learning: by individuals, by teams, by larger groups that together form the organization, and community learning, which cuts across boundaries.

3. Knowledge is either tacit or explicit. Both must be embraced to maximize learning. Sharing of tacit knowledge is harder—but essential.

4. Knowledge creation must be encouraged through refinements and through innovation.

5. Organizations must find a place—a Middle Way—between stagnation and chaos, where creativity thrives and is channeled to a practical end.

6. Four conditions must be met for accelerated organizational learning:

   • Creative tension between shared vision and acknowledged reality

   • Permeable organizational boundaries
   • Flexible resource architecture
   • Minimal rules

7. Too many rules can be stultifying. An accelerating organization needs a process by which new rules can be learned and weak or out-of-date rules shed.

8. New rules are best developed with the input of those who must apply them. But everyone should keep testing the rules and looking for better ones.

9. Remember the six main learning processes: two each for knowledge replication, knowledge adaptation and knowledge creation:

LEARNING	TECHNIQUE	TYPE
1. Transfer	Teaching	Replication
2. Internalization	Training	Adaptation
3. Sharing	Coaching	Replication
4. Codification	Systematizing	Adaptation
5. Refinement	Improvement	Creation
6. Innovation	Breakthrough	Creation

Learning Acceleration

Strategic Flexibility

Change–Readiness

Hidden Leverage

Operational Alignment

Organizational Involvement

LEARNING TO CHANGE AND CHANGING TO LEARN

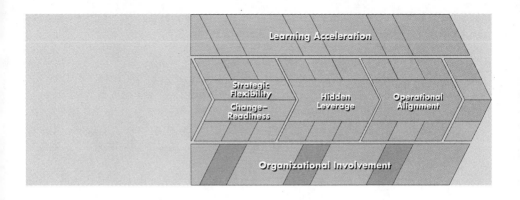

WHERE
DO YOU BEGIN?

Q: "How do I get to Blarney?"

A: "Mmm, if it's going to Blarney you're after, I wouldn't start
from here."

—OLD IRISH JOKE

We're often asked: "Where do I begin?"

The pragmatic answer is: "You start from wherever you are."

While development of a vision and strategy seem like the first
step in the process of change, if you already have a clear strategy
and the problem is how to implement it, you don't want to go
back to the strategy. Instead, you need to determine what the
points of leverage are to put your strategy into effect. If you
already know what those leverage points are, you should be concentrating on achieving operational alignment. You start wherever you are.

In the corporate world, change is hardly ever a green-field
operation. Almost invariably, the organization that needs to
change is already operating and must continue operating even
while it's being improved. Hence the dismay of managers facing a
cash crisis, when consultants tell them they must begin with a
new corporate vision to revive the firm. In our view, that advice
can be dangerously wrong.

The better approach is to focus first on those aspects of change that will bring the greatest short-term benefit without damaging the prospects for long-term improvement. To do that requires you to make the changes within a Relativistic framework like that proposed in this book. Provided that over time your organization moves forward on all fronts, it doesn't matter where you started—everything will be covered.

This philosophy becomes even more important when you realize that there's never only one thing that needs attention at any time. Many things require to be improved almost all the time: rethinking strategy, improving operations, resolving problems with people. A framework for change allows you to align all these activities.

The mission, always, is how to get to where your organization needs to be to cope with the never-ending changes of the foreseeable future. To develop an Accelerating Organization, you have to work on all the six aspects of transformation simultaneously, synchronously—and continuously.

Most people accept that they should continuously manage for learning acceleration and organizational involvement, but they assume that the other four components—managing for strategic flexibility, change-readiness, hidden leverage and operational alignment—are a sequence of phases. In the past they were. But not any more. Until recently a major change initiative had a start and an end. Broadly, you decided what you wanted, got ready for it, looked for hidden problems (if you were wise) and then implemented. The whole organization followed that sequence.

That no longer works: There's not enough time for the organization to pass all the way through the four phases before another initiative can be started. Change must be continuous, and the solution is not, as many assume, to execute the four phases faster and faster. Instead, change the mental model: All six processes are going on, to varying degrees, all the time.

Managing for organizational involvement and learning acceleration are, of course, permanent goals. But scanning the environment is also a continuous process, and so is testing the validity of strategies. Modifying scenarios and Relativistic strategies are intermittent—but far more frequent than the grand Newtonian strategy sessions of the past. Creating and reinforcing magnets is continuous, as is maintaining change-readiness. Understanding the unwritten rules that affect the organization must be never-ending (although that knowledge will be put to a variety of specific purposes). Finally, and notably, operational alignment must be a continuing process, even though each initiative will be implemented only once.

Remember always that it is the individual change initiatives passing through these processes that are intermittent—not the processes themselves. This is how to manage never-ending change: *Improve the change processes continuously and ferry one initiative after another through them.*

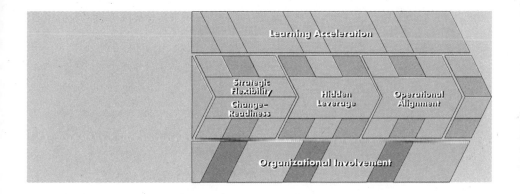

ADVANCING ON MANY FRONTS

The six continuous change processes cannot, clearly, be managed in isolation. They must be aligned with each other. That makes it easy for change programs to pass through them—and it ensures that the changes themselves are consistent and self-reinforcing.

And the more the changes reinforce themselves and each other, the more your organization will be able to learn how to come up with better changes faster, which will themselves reinforce the learning cycle, and so on. This is what creates an Accelerating Organization.

In such an organization, you must encourage many simultaneous efforts to improve different aspects of the management of the business—from strategy, to operations, to means of involving employees. And because all six change processes are continuous, you don't need to stop all action on operations improvement until someone has worked out the best way to accelerate learning. Nor do you have to put on hold projects to improve the learning infrastructure until the operations have been perfected. You can advance simultaneously on many fronts.

Indeed, you *must*. All the change processes are inextricably linked, even if you can separate them in your mind—and even though each process offers a unique perspective on an organization, a special way of looking into the complexity of organizational change, improvement and management.

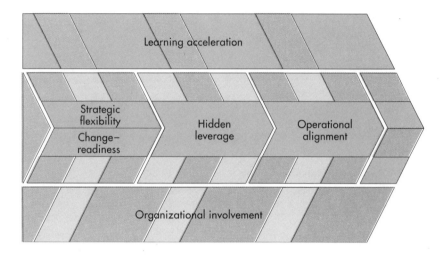

From each of these perspectives you can view the whole of the organization's workings. The concept of the Learning Organization, for example, is based on viewing an organization solely as a process of organizational learning. Or you can see an organization entirely as an enterprise for executing strategy, as many have done in the past. You can see the same organization as a series of operational business processes to be reengineered and aligned (the perspective taken in business process reengineering) or as a complex social system that can be improved by deeper organizational involvement (the philosophy of the O.D., or Organizational Development, school). You can even view the whole organization from the perspective of the unwritten rules that drive it.

While each of these perspectives is valid, relying on any one of them in isolation isn't very practical. It takes you in the direction of whatever fad is current; more importantly, it compounds the difficulty of achieving overall alignment. And without that alignment, the processes can fly apart.

A mental model of how change and learning occur, shared throughout the organization, avoids this disintegration—and ensures alignment. That's the scope of our approach: A model at once broad enough to encompass what everyone does, so that they can see where they fit in, but at the same time (using the principle of minimum critical specifications) guided by a few essential principles that leave people room to create new ways in their individual projects.

As shared mental models must be, the model in this book is designed to be easy to remember. You can break change into many more processes than the six we have, but in practice that's of little help. Psychologists have shown that at a given time people can keep in mind approximately seven things about any concept or activity. We suggest those seven should be the six change processes and managing the alignment among them.

Remember the acronym SCHOOL, to represent our six processes:

S trategic flexibility

C hange-readiness

H idden leverage

O perational alignment

O rganizational involvement

L earning acceleration

That's the model your organization must understand and follow.

■ AVOIDING BIG BANGS

To achieve large-scale transformational change, do you have to begin work on the whole organization at the same time? Emphatically, the answer is, "No!"

The wholesale adoption of new management ideas, packaged into universal panaceas and applied in predefined, precise steps, has been a principal reason for the failure of many TQM and Reengineering programs. It's likely to be a reason for the failure of prepackaged Learning Organization programs as well.

Allow us to inject some pragmatism into the frenzy of transformational change: If you view change as six processes that in due course need to be managed, you can select a menu of the right-sized chunks of change to proceed through—rather than risk choking to death by trying to swallow them whole. Although all six processes need to be improved—and must be aligned with each other as they are—they need not be tackled simultaenously. Instead, build up to it.

Let's face it: Every major consultancy these days is "taking the holistic view." That's all very well, and philosophically impeccable, but to most practical people it's impossible. To do everything that is suggested would massively overburden an already saturated workforce and undermine the organization it was intended to transform.

So as you contemplate changes, do not attempt everything at once. It's neither necessary, nor wise. And equally important, let your organization itself take responsibility for its change processes and the development of its own abilities. To do otherwise can be, at best, a short-term solution, at worst, an invasion that leaves an organization weak and dependent, unable to keep pace with the never-ending demands that will be thrown at it.

Outside advice and help should be welcomed where needed—and the more that is attempted, the more help may be needed—but that outside input should never be allowed to cut off an organization's ability to learn and to change.

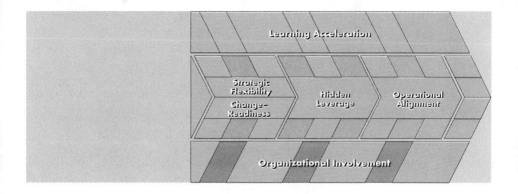

LETTING GO OF
SOME CONTROL

To maximize your organization's ability to advance as fast as possible on as many fronts as practical, you need to use all the energy of those people who want to make the organization more effective. It is thus essential that you not douse their enthusiasm by attempting to impose a centralized, mechanical control over the process.

In Chapter 1, we referred to Methuselah firms, companies that have survived hundreds of years by, among other things, allowing the divisions at their fringes to foray into new territory and try new strategies and organizational ideas, while the center maintained a stable core until the experiments proved successful and could be imported to the rest.

That strategy provides, in effect, the kind of safe-failing spaces that individuals and teams need for their local experiments. Be sure that these spaces for initial organizational experiments have three characteristics:

First, they must be sufficiently separated from the rest of the organization that they can change whatever they need to for their experiment—without the rest of the organization having to change itself in any significant way.

Second, they must be sufficiently similar to the rest of the organization for the experiment to have learning value for everyone.

Third, the leaders in the experimental site must have the desire and will to let people experiment and to change. They must be *change-ready*. Early experimenters with new ideas in an organization often have an intrinsic need to be different and out in front. These "self-starters" don't require any cranking. If there is a site in the corporation that needs change and could be a valuable learning experience for the rest of the organization, but doesn't have leadership with this self-starting ability, then new leadership of the right type will almost certainly be needed to make the site a valuable organizational learning opportunity.

 ## ENCOURAGING EXPERIMENTATION

At PepsiCo, a mental model of experimentation is encouraged. The vice chairman, Roger Enrico, says employees need the ability to break the rules: "To be able to think outside the box, not to be mesmerized by the limitations of the way things are done."

At AT&T, one fifth of its $3.5 million annual executive training budget is spent on courses that encourage introspection.

Leaders of change need to look for these three conditions, and encourage experimentation with new strategies and ideas at such sites. Sometimes, when a whole organization needs change and a sufficiently disconnected yet sufficiently similar site is not available, it may even need to buy a suitable company that offers the opportunity for the organization to observe closely and to experience an idea different from its own. After the acquisition, the CEO's task is to prevent the rest of the organization from smothering the differences in the name of standardization. The organization has to be made to see the acquisition as an opportunity to experiment with new ideas—and so to accelerate learning.

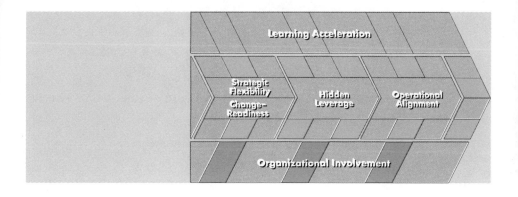

LEADING CHANGE AND LEARNING

Effective leaders must learn as their organizations learn. They can't stand apart and impart their wisdom, and thereby hope to create a Learning Organization. But, at the moment, there's a slight problem. Although many leaders have heard quite a lot about "the Learning Organization," most still have a rather confused idea of what it's all about.

On one recent occasion, a number of CEOs came together to discuss the subject. Almost everyone agreed that it was important and that to varying degrees they were all encouraging learning within their own organizations. Most of the CEOs then went on to talk about . . . training.

In other words, there's a lot of talk about learning that has little to do with Learning Organizations. So the first problem with encouraging leadership for change and learning is getting the leaders up to speed.

The second problem has to do with risk. Change is a risk for everyone, including an organization's leaders. Most top executives are loath to replace what has worked with something not yet tried or proven, even if there are good arguments for it. Just like everyone else, they need to be satisfied with answers to each of the five change-readiness criteria discussed in Chapter 2 People throughout the organization must feel that:

- Change is necessary
- The proposed change is appropriate
- As individuals, they have been acknowledged
- They have the skills to achieve the goals
- The "system" supports the required behavior

TOYOTA'S BELIEF IN PEOPLE

Toyota, the benchmark for the automobile industry in terms of quality and productivity, has achieved pre-eminence by focusing on the process of learning and improvement. Indeed, Toyota recently created a production line in an old factory in Japan that achieved even higher levels of quality—12 percent fewer defects and 20 percent higher productivity—than the company's previous best line. How did they do it?

They reduced the level of automation by two-thirds, putting more people back on the line. Toyota had learned that the machines and robots couldn't themselves learn and make further improvements. Only people could do that, provided they were given the right conditions and tools for learning. Toyota is confirming that rapid organizational learning is the ultimate competitive advantage—and that people are the critical core to that learning.

The third problem is attitude. A leader's desire to help create an Accelerating Organization needs to run far deeper than just a desire to sustain high performance. When we talk to leaders with a passion for creating accelerated learning, we sense a common view of what it is that unlocks the potential of an organization—it is people. Consider two examples.

At Tata, the Indian truck maker, former chairman Sumant Moolgaokar was very people-oriented, with great respect for the capacity of everyone in the organization to learn and master their disciplines. That came across in every encounter he had with people anywhere in his 40,000-person organization; he was a master of the art of Managing By Walking Around.

He would chat with operators of machines on the factory floor, with mechanics in the field, with gardeners on the company's grounds. He expressed interest in their lives and families—and he was always particularly curious about what people were learning about the work they were doing. He wanted to know what was new, what was better. He made people feel that their work was worthy, and that he was interested in their development and growth.

THE VOICE OF MOOLGAOKAR

"Men will believe in worthwhile goals. Times without number have I seen young men, fired by some such ideal, going far beyond the call of duty to make things happen. If what the organization stands for can evoke this spark in its people, it is on the way to achieving industrial progress. When men take pride in their skill or craft and strive to perfect it they give scope to their 'creative' impulses where one man's gain is not another's loss. It has long been established that people enjoy exercising their innate and trained abilities and that this enjoyment increases as the abilities become more complex. We can add nothing to this principle but we can certainly give it shape and make it come to life even in the industrial setting."

—*Sumant Moolgaokar, former chairman of the Tata Engineering and Locomotive Company, Ltd.*

Yet Moolgaokar and his managers and advisers had been taught to create boundaries and tight contracts and to provide incentives linked to those contracts. Tata was doing well—an endorsement for that approach. But Moolgaokar was uneasy with the contradiction: Giving individuals the freedom to learn and explore, as he did naturally in every one-on-one conversation, ran counter to the mechanistic way of managing them that underlay the management systems, which made him appear hard and impersonal. He was searching for management techniques in consonance with his personal values.

The solution came when a general manager began to explore new ways of managing people—forming cross-functional teams, abolishing individual incentives, and encouraging teams to set their own goals in line with the organization's objectives. Moolgaokar provided him protective cover from the corporate staff, which felt threatened by the innovations; he saw the emergence of a learning space for the organization, and for himself, too.

Within a couple of years, the experiment turned in dramatically better results than other parts of the already successful organization. So, others began to look for the lessons, in order to begin a process of change themselves. Moolgaokar reinforced this with his acknowledgement of what he had learned from the experiment about managing a large organization of people.

■ LEADING LEARNING AT CEMEX

Lorenzo Amaya, former managing director of Cemex's Pacific Division, tells a similar story: He and his team were enthusiastic about exploring the concepts of the socio-technical school as they designed a new plant, because they believed potential benefits were available that the efficient but mechanistic system in use could not realize.

The corporate staff made a strong case to the CEO, Lorenzo Zambrano, not to risk a major capital investment with an untested management system. Zambrano saw both the risk and the possibilities; when he had been a plant manager, he had successfully tried similar ideas on a smaller scale.

So he provided Amaya support for what Zambrano wisely described to the corporate staff as "an experiment." Because it was so categorized, Amaya was able to enlist the support of many members of the staff, all eager for a learning experience.

Much of the new way worked; some did not. But the result was that Zambrano and the rest of Cemex had more confidence in how to go forward with similar changes elsewhere.

Note how important the attitude of leaders is to this process. Leaders need to persuade themselves that risks are acceptable, then convey an attitude that emphasizes the importance of people.

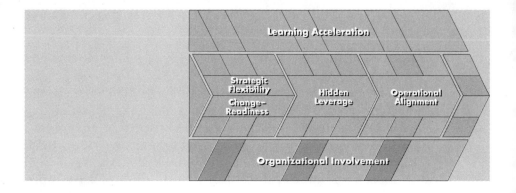

DOWNSIZING TO ACCELERATE

In an Accelerating Organization that is continuously changing, it's likely that new members will join and that many members will leave. The concept of lifetime employment with a single employer will be less relevant in such organizations.

On the one hand, as longevity has increased, many people wish to continue an active work life beyond the stipulated retirement age; on the other, organizations wish to provide room for their younger members to grow. And as many more people seek the freedom to sell their competencies to realize the maximum benefit for themselves—either because they want to or have been forced to—the concept of "employment" will also change, as it has begun to do for many. Perhaps organizations will some day learn how to manage the new social contract with their communities and with their members so that people can join and leave without trauma. But until they establish that ideal rhythm, they are likely to confront the need to dismiss a large number of people at one time, as they reengineer and downsize. The painful question for many leaders is how to manage this drastic step in ways that cause the least harm to the vitality and morale of the organization.

The criteria for organizational change-readiness provide a guide. When the organization has come to the point where major retrenchment is required, its employees have almost always recognized that change is necessary. Even if they have ideas themselves about what the solutions might be, they look for someone "to do something."

At such times, leaders can tap into the frustration and channel it into aspiration by sharing a vision of what the organization may become. So long as the vision of the process of change and improvement provides satisfying roles for employees, they may empower the leader to take charge. If the leader is seen as credible—which the leader can be only if he or she has been honest with employees about the problems, including how the leader may have contributed to them—this empowerment can provide a moral authority to lead on through the tough times ahead.

Acknowledgement is another important criterion of change-readiness, and it is here that leaders have the toughest calls to make. Roles may have to change in ways that disturb the status quo, and some people may have to leave the organization. It is best to do this firmly and expeditiously. But what about the pain?

 ## DOWNSIZING AT YPF

When the Argentine Government brought in new management at the national oil company, YPF, in 1990, its mandate was to reorganize the company to free it from the shackles of a state-run bureaucracy and to dramatically reduce the work force.

Through a broad range of programs that recognized people's needs and aspirations, YPF encouraged many workers to accept the changes it needed to make. The results were remarkable. Of 52,000 direct and contracted employees, more than 49,000 left. After some new employees were recruited, YPF was left with a highly motivated, skilled work force of not quite 6,000. After posting a loss of nearly $600 million (U.S.) in fiscal 1990, its earnings climbed to $706 million in fiscal 1993.

How was the change made with little labor strife and disruption? With an eye on the long term, through long negotiations with the powerful unions, and at considerable cost. First YPF negotiated the right to make layoffs by agreeing to pay substantial benefits to all displaced workers. More than 5,000 workers who were terminated were encouraged to start their own private companies, and YPF agreed to buy services from them for up to two years. For other employees, YPF provided a year of retaining at full salary, followed by severance payments.

YPF achieved a turnaround by acknowledging the human face of change.

Our advice is to acknowledge the human face of change as you make the tough decisions. Be fair, and acknowledge those who have been straining beyond the call of duty to help the organization move on. If you hurt them merely because you do not agree with them, the organization will lose respect for you and take away from you some of the moral authority it may have bestowed on you. Second, be firm. It is often tough for leaders to take the same action with the people immediately around them—other senior executives and their own personal staff—that they take with people in the organization with whom they are not personally connected. Such a double standard can diminish the leader's authority considerably and create a cynicism that is poisonous for the commitment required for any major change.

Chief executives of 40 European and Asian companies who gathered in Bombay in October 1995 to discuss the role of the CEO in transformational change confirmed this advice. Many recounted how their organizations would not rally behind them until they had taken the painful steps with their senior colleagues.

Be humane. Help those who have to leave as well as you can with outplacement services and generous severance packages. But, above all, let people leave with dignity. As a secretary in one organization undergoing major downsizing advised her managers: "We know some of us have to leave even though we have served here for decades. But do not take away our dignity now. We are human beings who did what we knew best. Times have changed, and admittedly some of us will not be able to learn the new skills required, and perhaps even if we could, we are too many. You do not have to shame us to leave, nor to impersonally show us the door. Let us part with respect for each other."

And finally, get on with it!

If the organization cannot be viable with all the people it now has, you are being counted on, even by them, to make the tough decisions. Check the financial implications and work through the legal implications, then move.

And always bear in mind that the need for traumatic downsizing is an indication of mismanagement in the past—of not learning to change flexibly and continuously. Let it be a lesson: the organization must refresh itself every day, every year. People must learn new skills, new teams should form and some people, or bits of the organization, may leave as others come aboard.

But this continuous change will not be traumatic in an Accelerating Organization, nor will it require the amputations that shock the organization and the surrounding community. If a downsizing is necessary, do it in a way that does not sap the resiliency of the organization. And, thereafter, manage the organization in ways that do not require further downsizings.

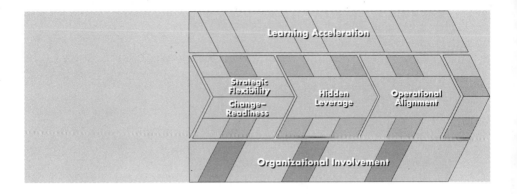

WHERE WILL YOU END UP?

For the last 20 years, organizations have become less intro-spective and more customer-oriented, less hierarchical and orga-nized more as horizontal "processes." In 1990, the Massachusetts Institute of Technology completed a five-year study of 100 firms in the automobile industry worldwide that described this new model of management. The study showed that the new approach had enabled certain Japanese firms to change how the industry com-peted. What's more, the new approach was not simply a manifes-tation of traditional Japanese culture, as some had described it, but rather the deliberate cultivation of a new way of managing complex organizations. And the authors of the study showed how this way of managing was being used outside Japan by some non-Japanese firms with dramatic results.

 MIT STUDY REFERENCE

The first findings of the MIT study were published in 1985 as a report, "The Future of the Automobile." Further research led to a book published in 1990, "The Machine That Changed the World" by James P. Womack, Daniel T. Jones and Daniel Roos (Rawson Associates, 1990).

In the last few years, American and European organizations, many of which have already benefitted from adopting several management approaches tested in Japan, have begun to look to the future. They want to find a way of managing that will enable Western companies to leap ahead of their Asian rivals in the next century. Of course, the leaders in the Asia Pacific region are looking for ways to remain at the forefront.

Whatever their starting points, nearly all these organizations envisage a future in which they will become more agile by networking across their boundaries and sharing their competencies, so providing their customers with much better and more economical service. They see the strong role information technology will play in enabling this networking, and they feel the need for standards of communications to facilitate easy networking. They also recognize the vital importance of people as their organizations' most appreciating assets.

The world seems to be moving inexorably toward networks of individuals and firms collaborating with each other—there is a clear consensus on that. In mid-1995, Arthur D. Little convened a gathering of senior executives whose companies had been rated by outside experts as the "Best of the Best" at managing organizations according to the new models. The group included DuPont, Hewlett-Packard, Corning, Xerox, MCI, Texas Instruments and others.

The executives who attended were each responsible for the development of programs of large-scale improvement. Each had extensive experience in business process reengineering or quality management; each also had strong views on how that should be done. It soon became clear that everyone shared a remarkably similar view of the evolution of management practices into the next century.

As these executives looked into the future, they saw an evolution from the relatively rigid, hierarchical, mechanistic organizations of today toward more flexible, adaptive, learning organizations in 10 years' time. What they all clearly recognized was that organizations had to be seen as part of their larger environments. And as they debated, a consensus arose about the principal changes that would take place in society that would pull organizations to work in a new networked fashion.

To create steps on a timeline to becoming a world-class accelerating organization in 2005, the participants divided their observations into three categories: management and organization, culture and people, and enabling or transition milestones.

The group concluded that high-performing organizations would move quickly in the next few years to identify not only competencies but also centers of excellence. They believed that a web structure—a network incorporating horizontal processes and company-wide functions such as information systems, accounting, human resources (described in Chapter 5)—would emerge soon, with centers of excellence at nodes on the web.

Further out, they expected alliances, the result of seamless information technology and relaxed regulatory control, to blur the boundaries of companies. The alliances themselves will be fluid, changing with changing strategic needs. And as a result, organizations will steadily get smaller, concentrating on competencies. Communications and information technologies will also accelerate the erasing of national boundaries for business. Concentration around competencies will drive outsourcing, which will lead to the creation of new markets in new places around the globe. The definition of jobs will change. Companies that are continuously learning will need people who learn continuously. Individual competencies will then be able to set up relationships with multiple organizations, further driving the notion of a virtual corporation.

While reflecting on the timeline they'd come up with, the participants of our think tank realized that managers would need to shift their mental models on the relationship between people and organizations.

The think tank concluded that with fewer people in full-time employment, and with fewer of those full-time employees expecting lifetime employment, the contractual relationship between firms and employees would radically change. The social contract is already changing—even in Japan—as firms reconfigure and change the relationship with their members so they can continue to reconfigure in a changing world.

The legal contract will have to change as well. Firms are addressing the social issues by preparing their employees to be more widely employable, providing them with more training and more marketable skills. They are even helping those who must leave to find other work.

Most employers continue to require employees to depart the firm leaving behind the new knowledge they generated with the firm—intellectual property, knowledge of customers, and so forth. The penalties for infringing these contracts are very severe, and the firms have the financial resources to pay for enormous legal fees that an employee can't afford.

Yet in a knowledge-based society, not just firms but also individuals will find their principal marketable asset is knowledge. Firms will appear more than a little duplicitous if they claim that they wish

A timeline for change

	1996–1997		
Management/ Organization	Internal performance measures linked clearly to external measures Firms focus on a few areas of competence CEO's role defined as integrator across processes and organizations; as negotiator/influencer	Evolution of common dynamic mental model and language in a company (vision, values, processes, markets) Flexible organization structures based on a network model applied by leading organizations	Centers of excellence emerge within corporation Recognition of the need to deal with people issues as success factor in reengineering
Culture/ People	Capitalizing on diversity 360-degree performance reviews Recognition that the way learning takes place needs to be changed; enable learning in organizations (e.g. in teams vs. individual)	High performance work systems: team-based, customer-focused Individuals specialize on their personal core competencies	
Society and Industry	Corporation begins to be understood as volume of transactions (not ownership of assets) Network technology for interoperability within and across corporations becomes available		

1998–2001		2002–2005	
Improved methods and tools to define core and outsourced/partnered opportunities	New improvement tools and techniques for creative processes	Improved work group tools give individuals greater access to systems	
Increased outsourcing and contracting of non-core competency processes	Quality becomes infused throughout company–less a part of the formal organization	Balanced organizational structure for central/decentral, process/function	
Processes designed to allow people flexibility in job content	Processes are redesigned to include elements of self-adaptive characteristics and elements of learning	Individual centers of excellence: corporation learning plans	
Overhauling of human resource organization from transaction management to pull-based support of operations		More self management vs. imposed management	
		More entrepreneurial organization	
Effective, skill-based evaluation systems		Telecommuting is accepted work mode	Changed relationship between individual and firm (empowerment and partnership)
Pay/rewards dependent on longer-term performance		Careers defined over a series of employers	
More flexible work rules		More emphasis on continual learning	Jobs/roles evolve to fit individuals' strengths
Value chains collapse; dynamic shifting of corporate boundaries in vertical value chain		Transaction standards	Relaxation of legal/governmental constraints to intercompany cooperation
		Accessible resource inventories	
		New definitions of financial attractive-ness and risk	More influence of corporations on education system (backward integration of supply chain)
		Multiple integrators scan and match competencies to form new partnerships and meet customers' requirements	

to help people to move on without trauma—unless they first relax their contractual agreements.

■ EVERYONE IS AT DIFFERENT STAGES

Talking with each other, the participants in the think tank found that each organization was at a different stage on the path to becoming a people-centered Accelerating Organization. Some had yet to take full advantage of the benefits to be accrued under the passing mental model of management. Some had moved on and were looking for the keys to unlocking changes that would allow them to thrive in the uncertainties of the next millennium—but the old mental models were still deeply entrenched and needed to change.

Others had moved even further, having made fundamental changes to their organizations and seeing early benefits. And everyone was curious about these new developments.

How would they prosper? Would they survive? Did they show promise of major benefits? At the same time, those who were experimenting at the frontiers of management practice wondered how to ensure that their developments delivered on the early promise they showed.

That's a pretty fair reflection of the range of starting points for organizations generally. The revolution we're all living through won't finish overnight; it will probably take 20 years before all but a few stragglers have made the transition to Accelerating Organizations.

■ SOFT FOR HARD AND HARD FOR SOFT

In the new school of management, "soft" processes are used to obtain hard results and "hard" frameworks to improve soft processes.

Vision, values, learning, involvement, trust and tacit knowledge are the soft constituents of the processes by which the Accelerating Organization achieves improvement in its ability to deliver and sustain high performance. It uses these soft yet vital ways explicitly, with hard, proven, logical techniques and tools. The new school aims for hard and sustainable business results— growth and profit—in the face of rapid and less predictable change. It roots its power in the aspirations of people who shape the world they want to live in and in their ability to learn, change and improve. It provides them the disciplines they must master to achieve their goals.

In this school, leaders have the 10 principal models we have described, offering a collection of techniques and tools to use to create a high-performing Accelerating Organization.

The models and tools complement each other. Visioning and Creative Tension, for example, dovetail into the Cascade of Magnets; Systems Thinking along with the M-E-T model provides insights into practical ways to spring the hidden levers; Teams within Networked Organizations along with Business Process Improvement create flexible and high-performing operational capabilities. Supporting each principal model are more detailed models and guidelines for action that have been described throughout this book.

**10 principal concepts and toolboxes for managing
the Accelerating Organization**

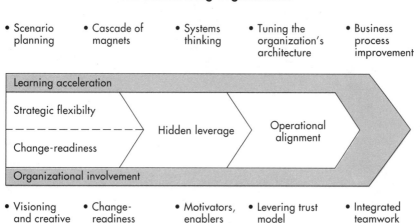

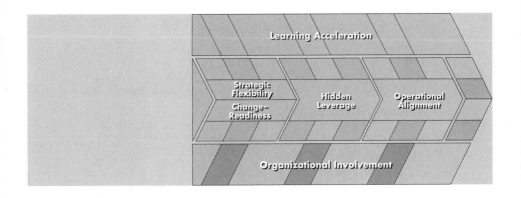

THE DAWN

So where does this all lead?

Here is our vision:

In the leading organizations of the Twenty-First Century, the six processes for learning to change and changing to learn will repeat themselves in the same pattern, sometimes narrower, sometimes wider, resonating within the organization, rippling outward. Societies, organizations within societies, teams within those organizations and individuals within the teams will all follow the same path and the same principles of learning and change that we've looked at.

The six sets of management goals—our SCHOOL of Strategic flexibility, Change-readiness, Hidden leverage, Operational alignment, Organizational involvement and Learning acceleration—will hold true in every environment: factories, partnerships, corporations, cooperatives, virtual organizations, nonprofit organizations, civil services and governments. All will need to learn to change and change to learn.

There are many reasons for us all to aspire to be part of such Accelerating Organizations. Some reasons are business-oriented—the bottom lines, or whatever else management is interested in, will look very good. Others are more intangible—such organizations will be exciting places to work, for instance. Perhaps most important is that Accelerating Organizations will find they become more and more responsive to fluctuations in their industries and signals from their customers and suppliers. And that is the strongest defense against an unknowable future, for organizations and people alike.

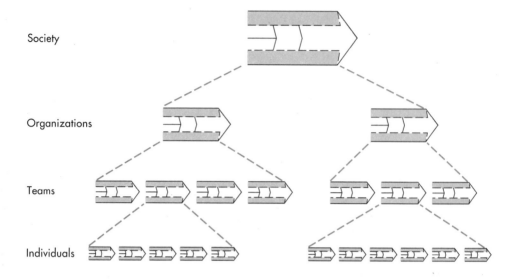

Society

Organizations

Teams

Individuals

THE NEW DAWN WILL FEEL DIFFERENT

Can we doubt that the successful organizations of the early Twenty-First Century will be very different from most organizations today?

Fear and blame will have ceased to be the core management tools, as they currently are. Aspiration and organizational learning will have replaced them. Upper management will no longer attempt to control other employees, forgoing the mental model that employees, left to their own devices, will not do what the executives want. Indeed, centralized control will largely be gone, compensated for by shared visions of a future to which people feel a personal connection and that they want to turn into reality, as well as by core values that the organization holds dear. Managers will be expected to support rather than control.

XEROX AND NEVER-ENDING CHANGE

"We believe our competitive advantage lies in a fully empowered workforce that can quickly adapt to change. That is our only competitive advantage."

—*Norman E. Rickard, president, Xerox Business Systems.*

The environment will continue to change and flex in an unpredictable fashion. The Accelerating Organizations will anticipate with scenarios, respond at the first signals that a scenario is in fact occurring, then rapidly change to take maximum advantage of the shift.

But people throughout the organizations will no longer suffer from change fatigue because they will be agents of change rather than its victims: The body of the organization will pull the change through, rather than top management trying to aggressively push the change. Lasting change will emerge from within the hearts and minds of employees who aspire together to create something different, better, greater.

And management focus will shift: In addition to managing according to the formal, official aspects of a business, everyone will take account of the unwritten rules driving their organization. They will regularly look at the big picture—even bigger than the unclear boundaries to their own organization—and try to see the pattern of invisible systemic connections. They'll then focus on potential leverage points to understand exactly what's driving them. Where appropriate, they'll home in on those points and change the bare minimum needed to effect the results they need.

Major episodic change initiatives will be superseded. In their place will be a stream of major overlapping initiatives, ferried through the six continuous change processes that ensure overall alignment and reinforcement. The organization structure that reinforces such alignment will be a fan of semi-permanent processes, overlaid by fluid teams that coalesce and disband as needed. And the outcomes of the changes will no longer be measured primarily in financial terms, but by a portfolio of measures that include leading indicators of what is likely to lead to high performance.

Interactions within the best organizations will, for most people, be different from anything that has occurred in a working environment in living memory. Conversations will balance advocacy and inquiry, people will attempt to share the logic behind their assumptions, and there will be far less management and peer pressure to produce short-term, local action items from each and every meeting.

Instead there will be a strong desire to make fundamental improvements—innovative changes that will help the organization as a whole to keep reinventing itself. And such creativity will be expected to emerge from a variety of experiments throughout the organization—only a few of which will be expected to succeed.

Above all else, the successful organizations of the future will embrace the human face of change in everything they do, not out of altruism or caring or political correctness, but from hard-nosed pragmatism. Because people are the organization's fastest-appreciating assets.

 LIFELONG LEARNING AT MOTOROLA

"We believe strongly in the concept of lifelong learning. In the Information Age, people are the only real assets, and education is the key to quality, productivity and sustained profitability."

—*Gary L. Tooker, vice chairman and CEO, Motorola.*

A NEW BEGINNING

Does it all sound revolutionary?

Well, this is revolt, against the established management practices that have served for two centuries. A revolt against the ineffectiveness and inhumanity that those mechanistic approaches often brought. It will touch every corner of our lives. For this is not just a revolution of the workplace, but a revolution of every organization in society.

The dawn of the next millennium will see the dawn of a new age. When most of us are retired, we will look back on our part in that fundamental transition in the way humanity worked, interacted and lived. We will remember how, toward the end of the Twentieth Century, a few organizations dared to take a leap of faith. And how those that did prospered. And how, over the next 20 years, almost every organization in every society made that same transition.

And we'll remember how, from the shadows of the old century, one organization after another held hands—and leaped into the light.

INDEX

ABOUT THE AUTHORS

Arun Maira is an internationally recognized authority on the practices of organizational change and performance improvement. He is managing director of Innovation Associates, the company co-founded by Peter Senge that is the leading provider of consulting technology in organizational learning, and is also leader of Arthur D. Little's worldwide Organizational Transformation and Learning Practice. Maira has led major programs of organizational transformation all over the world for 30 years, both as an executive and a consultant.

Peter Scott-Morgan is a globally recognized authority on understanding and removing barriers to change and corporate learning, and is in frequent demand as a speaker on business management topics. He is Worldwide Director of Learning at Arthur D. Little, where for more than a decade he has worked with top managers of major corporations around the world to help them accelerate high performance. Dr. Scott-Morgan is the author of the best-selling *Unwritten Rules of the Game (McGraw-Hill, 1994)*.